THE TEAM COACHING TOOLKIT

55 Tools and Techniques for Building Brilliant Teams

by

Tony Llewellyn

First published in Great Britain by Practical Inspiration Publishing, 2017

© Tony Llewellyn, 2017

The moral rights of the author have been asserted

ISBN (print): 978-1-910056-65-3
ISBN (ebook): 978-1-910056-64-6 (Kindle)
ISBN (ebook): 978-1-910056-73-8 (ePub)

All definitions come from the Apple online dictionary unless otherwise specified.

Trademark notice: Product or corporate names may be trademarks or registered trademarks and are used only for identification and explanation without intent to infringe.

Practical Inspiration
PUBLISHING

To Sian, Angharad, Rhiannon and Bryony

CONTENTS

How to use this book..xi

SECTION ONE – The Theory 1

Chapter 1 – Introduction 3

Chapter 2 – Using tools to shape team dynamics 13

Chapter 3 – The emergence of the team coach....................................23

SECTION TWO – Team Coaching Techniques....................................37
Technique 1.   Systemic thinking and the spheres of influence................39
Technique 2.   Facilitating a thinking environment 43
Technique 3.   Slow down to speed up 46
Technique 4.   Curious enquiry 50
Technique 5.   Influential questions 53
Technique 6.   Listening for clues 56
Technique 7.   Adopt an 'Agile' mindset 59
Technique 8.   Using case stories 62
Technique 9.   The importance of visual information................................65
Technique 10.   Developing your maturity in complexity............................69

SECTION THREE – Team Coaching Tools 73

Chapter 4 – Tools for assessing the team's environment 75
    1.   Is your project complex or simply complicated?.............................76
    2.   Assess the project environment 78
    3.   Articulating stakeholder paradoxes 81
    4.   The 'cup of tea meeting' 84

v

5. Celebrating cultural diversity 86
6. Dangerous assumptions and leaps of faith 89
7. Roles not jobs 92
8. Force field analysis 95
9. Surviving the storming stage 98

Chapter 5 – Tools for setting up an effective team **101**
10. The Big 'Why?' 102
11. Extrovert and introvert thinking 105
12. Learning from the past 108
13. Establishing your rules of engagement 110
14. Agreeing to take feedback 113
15. Building a future story 116
16. How to motivate or annoy me 118
17. The collaboration canvas 121
18. Create an awareness of behavioural gravity 124
19. Establish a 'no blame' culture 127
20. The Team Integration Manual 130

Chapter 6 – Tools for improving communication **133**
21. Establish a collaboration and integration workstream 134
22. The language of collaboration 136
23. Building a team psychometric profile 139
24. Everyone speaks, everyone is heard 142
25. Systemic problem-solving model 144
26. Who plays the fool? 146
27. The 'so what?' monitor 148
28. Agree your meeting strategy 150
29. Identifying the elephant 153
30. Perceptual positions from the 'extra chair' 156
31. Building stakeholder support 158

Contents

Chapter 7 – Tools for building resilience..**161**

   32. Press reset 162

   33. Taking the resilience temperature 166

   34. Constructive challenge 169

   35. Coping with difficult news 172

   36. Fault free conflict management and the 'Evil Genius' 175

   37. Hedges and potholes 178

   38. The pre-mortem: An alternative approach to risk management..................... 181

Chapter 8 – Tools for encouraging learning, innovation and improvement **185**

   39. The midpoint review 186

   40. Knowledge stocktake.. 188

   41. Capturing the knowledge 190

   42. How are we performing? Team key performance indicators........................... 192

   43. Lifting the barriers to allow creative thinking 196

   44. Running a successful 'lessons learned' session 198

   45. Purposeful closure 201

SECTION FOUR – What next? **203**

Chapter 9 – Reading list and other resources 205

References.. 207

ILLUSTRATIONS

FIGURES

Figure 1 – The foundation layers of an effective team 16

Figure 2 – Team coaching model 74

Figure 2A – Team coaching model: Assess the environment 75

Figure 2B – Team coaching model: Set-up 101

Figure 2C – Team coaching model: Communicate 133

Figure 2D – Team coaching model: Build Resilience 161

Figure 2E – Team coaching model: Improvement and learning 185

Figure 3 – The spheres of influence 40

Figure 4 – Assess the project environment 79

Figure 5 – Examples of typical project paradoxes 82

Figure 6 – An example of a Force Field Analysis 96

Figure 7 – Introvert–extrovert continuum 107

Figure 8 – Illustration of good meeting/bad meeting exercise 111

Figure 9 – Set up for the motivate or annoy me exercise 119

Figure 10 – An example of a collaboration canvas 122

Figure 11 – Illustration of behavioural gravity 125

Figure 12 – 'No blame' protocol 128

Figure 13 – Enquiring versus controlling language styles 136

Figure 14 – Constructive challenge cycle 170

Figure 15 – Kübler-Ross change curve 172

Figure 16 – Fault free conflict resolution process 176

Figure 17 – Hedges and potholes 179

TABLES

Table 1 – The foundation layers of the team building process 17

Table 2 – Real team checklist 18

Table 3 – A changing approach to project management 30

Table 4 – Complicated or complex 77

Table 5 – Alternative approaches to gaining feedback 115

Table 6 – Meeting strategy guide 150

Table 7 – Examples of Key Performance Indicators found to have an impact on team behaviour 194

HOW TO USE THIS BOOK

This book is a toolkit to help you build better teams. It is therefore designed to be a quick reference guide for team leaders and team coaches to find a tool or technique that will be useful in a particular situation.

The book is structured around 10 team coaching techniques, and 45 team coaching tools. I have also provided three preliminary chapters which will give you some background to the art and science of team coaching.

Creating something new, or fixing something that is broken, usually requires finding the best tool to do the job. In the same way that it would usually be better not to try and open a tin of paint with a sharp chisel, it is worth taking some time to understand what each tool is intended to achieve. You can then decide how you might adapt it to suit your current needs.

The toolkit is set out according to a model of coaching teams engaged in some form of project or initiative. The model provides a progression through five phases of a team's life cycle.

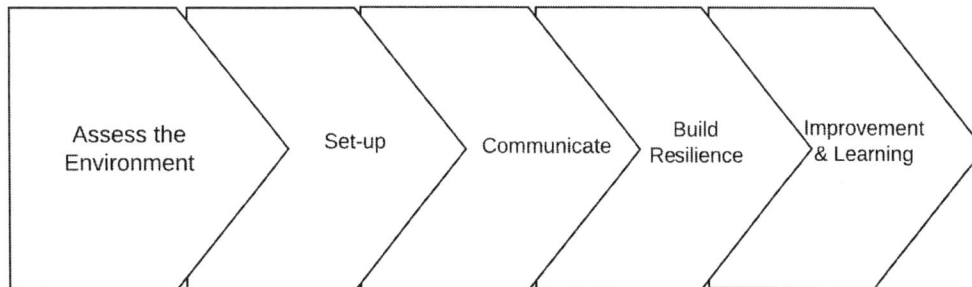

Team Coaching Model

This model is explained in chapter 3, but you will quickly be able to recognize which tools fit within which stage of the model as each is referenced to the above image.

There is a companion website teamcoachingtoolkit.com where you can download some of the charts and tables used in some of the tools.

These tools have a degree of flexibility in their application. Experiment and adapt them to fit your situation and your style of working. Good luck and if you have any questions or comments, contact me at to.llew@mac.com. I would love to hear how they work for you.

Tony Llewellyn
Hertfordshire
England

May 2017

SECTION ONE  The Theory

CHAPTER 1

INTRODUCTION

This is a book about team building. It doesn't have much to say about white water rafting, building temporary structures from wood or string, or the merits of taking everyone to the pub. Instead the focus is on how to engage with a group of individuals and form them into a collaborative and productive unit. The tools and techniques set out in the following pages may provide less instant gratification, but are more likely to be successful in building an engaged, committed and resilient team.

Team building is a scientific process, involving the methodical application of a series of steps. You are, however, dealing with human beings rather than machines, and so the process requires a more subtle approach. In a situation where people are needed for their spirit and ingenuity, then attention must be paid to the psychological forces that shape relationships.

WHO SHOULD READ THIS BOOK?

The book is written for anyone whose role is to support and sustain a productive and functioning team. You may be a project manager, pulling together a collection of technical specialists to create a piece of software or to construct a new building. Alternatively you may be in a management role in a large organization and have been tasked with leading a cross-functional team to deliver an important initiative. The toolkit is also likely to be of interest to team coaches and facilitators who are brought in to provide support that will enable the team to establish the process and behavioural norms associated with team effectiveness. Whatever your role, the toolkit is designed to prove a number of activities that have been found to get your team thinking, talking and working together as a single unit rather than a collection of individuals.

The book is structured in three parts.

Section One sets out some useful background information into team dynamics and the processes that have been necessary to build a group of disparate individuals into a real team. The first chapter covers some of the primary elements of group interaction and gives the reader an understanding of the framework around which a leader needs to build his/her team. The second chapter looks at the growing development of team coaching and sets out some of the theoretical and practical ideas that underpin team coaching either as an activity in its own right or as a style of leadership.

Section Two introduces 10 techniques upon which to build your team coaching practice. A technique can be defined as a skilful way of doing or achieving something. I have stretched the definition to include a way of approaching the challenges of team coaching which are as much about your philosophy or mindset as they are about physical action.

Section Three moves into the toolkit, setting out 45 different 'tools' or activities you may find useful in working with your team. These tools are set out in a structure that follows the sequential logic of team building that is explained in chapter 3.

Much research has been done on team development and some of this thinking is included in the following chapter. There are some great books and articles available, a selection of which I have listed in the closing chapter. These publications will help you learn *why* teams are important and *what* needs to be done to build an effective team. This book takes the progression a bit further and sets out *how* you go about the team building process.

This is not an academic book but I have tried where possible to explain some of the theory that supports both the tools and techniques. My purpose is to give you a sense of why the proposed activity is necessary or useful, as well as providing you with some context, either for your own satisfaction or to explain to the team. The theory is generated from numerous studies into team development and where appropriate I have supplied references for further reading. Some of these tools are my own inventions whilst others are adapted from my research or have been suggested by other friends and collaborators working in the field of team development.

GREAT TEAMS ARE RARE

I have spent much of the last five years talking to experienced managers about life in work teams, and listening to their stories. Most people have at least one great team experience that stands out in their memory. When they tell their story it comes across clearly and vividly, often told with a gentle smile on their face as they recall people and events from the past. I have heard similar tales told multiple times by different people with different professional backgrounds and from different countries. Great team experiences can be life enhancing. People who have worked in a strong team rarely forget it. They describe the way that time just seemed to fly past. Everyone had a clear sense of direction, knew what they needed to do and when they needed to step in to help others. The odd thing about these stories is that they are often presented as singular events, as if they reflect an unusual set of circumstances that are rarely repeated.

My research indicates that most of our team experiences are much less satisfying. For many, teamwork is a notional term for working alongside others with no clear sense of purpose and limited clarity around what needs to be done or by whom. I have collected many stories of disconnected leadership, inadequate communication and low group morale. For some people a bad team experience can be emotionally scarring. It can push individuals to change industries, or even to decide to change careers.

It raises the question, '*why are great team experiences so difficult to replicate?*' What are the critical factors that have been found to influence whether groups of people work together effectively, or simply drift through their working lives waiting for something better to happen? As we will see, there are many elements that contribute to a great team, some of which are practical procedures that can be identified and put in order. Others require the development of a broader set of techniques. This book works through a number of these components and sets out some practical proposals that will help you set up and maintain a strong team. Before we get into the detail, it is first worth considering a few matters that establish the context of the discussion ahead.

SOCIAL ANIMALS

The subject of teams and teamwork has engaged the minds of a wide range of scholars and practitioners and has generated a vast amount of literature over the last 50 years. The field incorporates thinking from such diverse disciplines as psychology, organizational behaviour, sociology and education. Humans as a species are generally social animals. We find both safety and comfort, as well as creativity and energy, by working with others and have been doing so for many thousands of years. It is perhaps a little surprising then that so much thought and attention has been put into studying what is surely just a natural phenomenon.

If all groups functioned effectively in the same way, or alternatively, every attempt by people to collaborate ended in failure, we would perhaps be less interested. The peculiar thing is that in some circumstances groups and teams achieve great things and other times they do not. Sometimes teams have been found to be better at task completion, decision-making, learning and problem-solving. Other studies find that groups are less adept at these processes. Why is that? Surely we have been practising teamwork for long enough as a species to have worked out the processes by now.

The problem of course is that people are messy. We are not consistent. Our behaviour towards other humans is governed as much by emotion as it is by rational thought. Emotions are difficult things to work with. They are generated by minds that are rarely in full control, and can change unpredictably. And yet this emotional component of team behaviour is the one area that has had relatively limited study, largely I suspect, because the complexity of human emotions makes scientific examination rather difficult.

So whilst there are no clear rules for regulating behaviour in groups, there has been enough research, observation and analysis to arrive at a set of guidelines, which might be considered to be best practice. Many of these common success factors are presented as standard instructions in a range of managerial textbooks. However, despite all of the advice on leadership, team development, and people motivation that is available to us, most of our team experiences fail to reach that golden moment of team synergy where the collective output of the team exceeds the sum of its parts.

It is easy to be cynical. Human beings are often unreliable, unpredictable and selfish. Ideas about teamwork and collaboration can sometimes be dismissed as simply wishful thinking. And yet most people have experienced working in at least one great team, where the group worked together with energy and commitment. When people tell me their stories of great teams I ask them to try and describe what made the difference. Often they're not really sure and rationalize the outcome as the fortunate combination of naturally collaborative individuals. As I dig down into their story, however, it becomes clear that whilst luck may be playing a part, the basic elements of successful teams are revealed time and time again.

As we will discuss later, however, in many ways the odds are stacked against the creation of an effective team. The dark side of human nature does not cope well with the challenges of ambiguity and uncertainty that are a common feature of today's workplace. I have collected other less inspiring tales of poor leadership, internal conflict and failed outcomes. The memories of frustration, stress and anger are often painful to recall and yet they continue to occur without us seeming to be able to learn to find an alternative.

It doesn't have to be this way. Bad team experiences should not be the default expectation. There are enough studies on team performance to identify a strategy and then implement a plan to consistently build and maintain energetic, creative and strongly bonded teams. I believe therefore that great team experiences can be replicated. The key is to understand the different success factors and learn to apply them. Some of these factors are a simple matter of good organization and planning. Others, however, are less obvious and consequently need deeper consideration. It is this opaque aspect of team development that we will focus on though the book.

JUST ANOTHER BOOK ON TEAMS?

This book began life as a hobby. I have been collecting tools and techniques for working with teams for a number of years in my work as a team coach, facilitator, trainer and consultant. One day I decided, on impulse, to build a website called the Team Coaching Toolkit. (If you have not already visited the site check out www.teamcoachingtoolkit.com) The site is designed specifically to provide team leaders and project managers with a place to find new ideas and tools to develop their teams, and contains some of the tools and techniques set out in this book. I had recently been introduced to the concept of 'working out loud', in an article by Harold Jarche (2015), and was intrigued by the idea that instead of hoarding your own ideas as some form of intellectual property you should share them, to see how other people might make them bloom.

The internet has radically changed how one person's thinking can be disseminated and adapted. We are able to quickly build networks of contacts and collaborators working in a diverse range of sectors and industries. This sharing philosophy is based on a recognition that, as a single human, my ability to have an influence on the thinking and mindset of others is inevitably limited to those with whom I work face to face. My ambition is to have a greater impact. By publishing these tools, techniques and other information on team development, either in print or online, I hope to stimulate you and others to try them and build your own capability in creating effective, cohesive teams.

I believe that team building skills are really important. The scale and complexity of the world's challenges are simply too great for individuals to tackle alone. The caricature of the heroic leader who will bravely step up and save the day is increasingly defunct. Most successful leaders are clear that their accomplishments are primarily the result of the efforts of a group of people working together as a unit. Teamwork is often extolled in books and articles on improving organizational performance. I have found, however, that for all that leaders talk about building a great team, most have little idea around the execution of a team development plan. Many managers would like to create a strong and vibrant team environment, but few know how to go about it.

The problem is that team building is often a slow process. As we will see, it takes time and energy both of which are in short supply in a culture when 'urgency' tends to override the 'important'. In my research I have found that too many managers rely on a strategy of hope, and assume that as long as everyone does their job, an effective team will suddenly emerge. This complacent view will not be enough for the teams of the future. We live in changing times. The certainties that we used to be able to rely on are slowly disappearing. Writing in 2017, the political structures that sustained us through a period of growth and prosperity appear to be falling apart, leaving us in a highly uncertain environment where decisions must be made with no clear sense as to how the 'law of unintended consequences' will affect our future.

Economic cycles in which activity speeds up and slows down are becoming shorter. We can no longer rely on steady periods of growth upon which to make long-term investment decisions. Most organizations around the world are struggling to cope with the disruption created by the emergence of new technology. The potential efficiencies offered by the digital revolution are creating new winners, whose business models will start to dominate different economies around the world. The disruption is, however, causing significant stress in many established institutions. Recent advances in computing power are set to create even more turmoil as innovators find new and increasingly powerful ways of using data and developing artificial intelligence.

All of this change requires teams to find ways of adapting and then implementing programmes to whatever turns out to be the new normal. No one individual has the knowledge or experience to know how to adjust to this new reality. Organizations small, medium and large are all being forced to implement projects and change initiatives to work out how they can adapt. Many talk about the need for transformation but that is potentially misleading as it implies the shift from one steady state to another. In the immediate future it is difficult to identify what a steady state would look like.

There is an increasing sense that the old hierarchal structure which was used to manage 'business-as-usual' is becoming increasingly out of date. Many people now spend their working life engaged in projects rather than running the day-to-day business activities. And projects need teams. Difficult projects need very good teams and to build good teams takes skill, patience and a change in mindset.

SOFT SKILLS

Team development requires investment in the soft skills which turn out to be quite hard to develop. The command and control culture of the 20th century required little in terms of communication and empathy skills. All that managers needed to learn was how to give orders and rebuke subordinates who failed to achieve what had been intended. The complexity of the 21st century requires leaders who can stimulate discussion, find innovative solutions and inspire coordinated action. Developing those skills is, however, likely to be a good long-term investment. For all the technological advances we are likely to see in the next 20 years, it is unlikely that big data or artificial intelligence will be able to replace the critical role of moving the hearts and minds of a collection of human beings to bring them together as a cohesive team.

Interacting with other human beings requires an ability to connect at a level that will enable a team to work alongside each other in an effective manner. Unlike hard skills, which are typically technical or knowledge-based, soft skills encompass a range of features which include empathy, problem-solving, adaptability, reciprocation, conflict management and collaboration. Looking at this list, one can see why the term soft is used to describe them. The challenge in trying to master any one of these areas is that they are context specific. In other words, how you apply a particular skill will vary according to the situation. Soft skills are unlikely to be learned solely by reading textbooks. They are principally learned through practice.

In essence, most soft skills are contained within the concept of communication. Skilful communication is not merely the ability to speak or present well. Real communication requires a level of prediction as to how the recipient of your information is likely to make sense of the messages they receive. In other words, to understand how you will receive my message, I first need to know more about you. The ability to draw information out of people is a valuable skill in its own right. Some people have a natural inquisitiveness and within 10 minutes of meeting a stranger will learn many details of the personal life of their new acquaintance. For most of us, however, enquiry is not a natural skill, nor is it one we are encouraged to develop. In a command and control environment, communication is generally a one-way process. The transactional management approach is based on directive activity. People are told what to do, without much genuine interest as to what they think or understand.

There is a paradox in that many large organizations invest huge sums of money in soft skills training which the underlying culture cannot really value. New knowledge of the potential ways to improve communication is never practised and so the learning does not become embedded.

The course notes are placed in a drawer never to see the light of day again. In a complex environment the nature of the game changes. Since managers can no longer accurately predict the future, it becomes more difficult to rely on one-way communication. In a 'sense and react' culture, the effective two-way exchange of information becomes critical to the organization's ability to adapt and thrive.

Real two-way communication therefore underpins virtually every process described in this book. As you read on, think about your current communication abilities and the extent to which you feel they could be improved.

BUILDING THE TEAM YOU NEED

The toolkit is designed to help you build the team you need. In the same way that a craftsman uses tools to cut, bind and mould a piece of material into the shape he wants, this toolkit has been written to help you craft a group of individuals into an effective team. You can leap straight into the toolkit sections and find a technique or tool that you need for a specific event or purpose.

If you have more time, however, you may find it helpful to understand a bit more about team dynamics and how the coaching process makes use of tools to influence human beings to build the relationships that are fundamental to good teamwork. These are discussed in the next two chapters.

Chapter 2

USING TOOLS TO SHAPE TEAM DYNAMICS

This book is designed as a toolkit that will help you mould a group into an effective and productive unit. If you are going to try and shape a team, it is worth taking some time to understand the nature of team dynamics, how they emerge and then shift over time. This chapter provides a basic insight into the human factors that will ultimately affect whether you are successful. We look first at the topic of team dynamics, and the need to pay attention to behavioural norms. This section also sets out the foundational structure for team building and then considers how the tools work in establishing the right behaviours.

GROUP DYNAMICS

Humans use many forms of communication that do not require the interpretation of words to send or receive messages. Our eyes, facial muscles, voice tone, posture and arm movements all provide clues as to how we are feeling when we are part of a group. When such body movements are extreme, the messages can be quite obvious. Angry eyes or a sulky posture are easy to detect, but most of the activities that we call body language are often only detected at a subconscious level. This is just one aspect of the many behavioural clues that are there to be seen if you choose to look for them.

The word dynamics as applied to a group can be defined as the 'forces which stimulate growth, development or change within a system or process'. When we talk about group dynamics we are frequently thinking about the tensions that are sensed as being present in the room without being able to articulate exactly what those tensions are. These forces can be positive or negative, but will usually be a mixture of both. The dynamics of the group are integral to the way that its members interact. Positive group dynamics well help create a discussion that is energized and open. Negative dynamics are usually driven by fear and will cause people to be cautious and withhold information. Learning to read the room and sense the sources of support or disruption can make a significant difference to your ability to influence the team's effectiveness.

As mentioned in the previous chapter, unless you take active steps to build a positive attitude in the team, the default tendency of groups is to move towards dysfunctional relationships. It is helpful to recognize the primary factors that will lead to a breakdown in communication. We casually talk about dysfunctional families or dysfunctional groups without having a clear sense as to just what the phrase actually means. When applied to a team, the word dysfunctional could be associated with a group who are no longer connecting or communicating according to the behavioural norms of that particular group.

IT IS ALL ABOUT THE NORMS

Dysfunctional is nevertheless a relative term. Positive group norms are the result of the often subconscious acknowledgement of what behaviours each member of a team is prepared to accept if they are going to be emotionally and intellectually engaged in the team's activities. The team stops functioning effectively when one or more members are no longer prepared to commit emotionally to the rest of the team. To avoid the tendency towards dysfunction, a team may need help to actively work out what norms must be established to achieve the required collective output.

A norm is 'a standard or pattern, especially of social behaviour, that is typical or expected'. So norms are less about what we do and more about the way that we do them. When a group of individuals come together to work on an initiative or project, each will arrive with their own behavioural baggage. The fascinating thing about groups and teams, however, is that the norms acquired from working in other groups do not necessarily transfer to the new team.

Behavioural norms will vary from group to group. For some groups, low levels of communication are seen as perfectly adequate for their needs. For example, a team of introverts may be very successful, working together with a limited amount of interaction. Their personal need for communication may be focused solely around the completion of the task, and so other forms of social exchange are less important to them. Other teams thrive on high volume face-to-face interaction, where vigorous debate and disagreement are a part of the team's way of doing their work.

It is important to understand that norms are not simply about manners. Manners are a form of social construct. They are usually cultural and are often implicit. Whenever a group of relative strangers meet for the first time you will observe a tendency for most people to hold back and observe what is happening in the group. This is a natural mechanism for self-preservation as we assess the group and work out how we are likely to fit. So new groups start off behaving in a way that might be described as polite. However, just because you observe someone being calm and polite when you first encounter them does not mean they will automatically share the same cultural norms. A common mistake made by many team leaders is to assume that the polite and attentive behaviours they observe in the group when it first meets will be sustained throughout the project. Consequently, they spend insufficient time setting the right norms only to find that difficult behaviours quickly emerge once the team moves into action. As the leader/coach you have the opportunity to establish a new set of norms that may be quite different. Each group has their own set of unwritten rules as to 'how things are done here'. The coaching skill is to make those rules explicit rather than assumed. This leads us to the concept of team building.

BUILDING THE EMOTIONAL FOUNDATIONS

The term *team building* is a familiar phrase. It may conjure up a range of emotions. For some, the words may imply time spent out of the office being paid to have fun with your co-workers. For others, the image may be distinctly different, recalling memories of being coerced into carrying out irrelevant exercises whilst risking the disdain and ridicule of one's colleagues. Building a real team has relatively little to do with outdoor pursuits or time spent eating and drinking at the firm's expense. Whilst such activities may help teammates learn more about each other's social existence outside of work they are a poor substitute for a structured team development process. Process can be described as 'a series of actions or steps taken in order to achieve a particular end'. Team process has two distinct strands: i. Task accomplishment processes that are used by the team to carry out their day-to-day work involving such things as the allocation of resources, programming and reporting; and ii. People engagement processes designed to create awareness, build trust and set behavioural norms.

Task accomplishment tends to be specific to the proposed objective. This is where most managers and leaders devote the majority of their energy in the early days of the team's existence. It is vital to recognize that 'people engagement' requires that same level of priority as it provides the foundations for the transition from a workgroup to a real team. Spending too little time on engagement in the early phases of a team's life will almost certainly require more energy taking remedial measures later on. In fact, the reverse is true in that time invested in setting the right behavioural norms early in the project cycle will save time later as the team build up speed. (See **Technique 3** – 'Slow down to speed up'.)

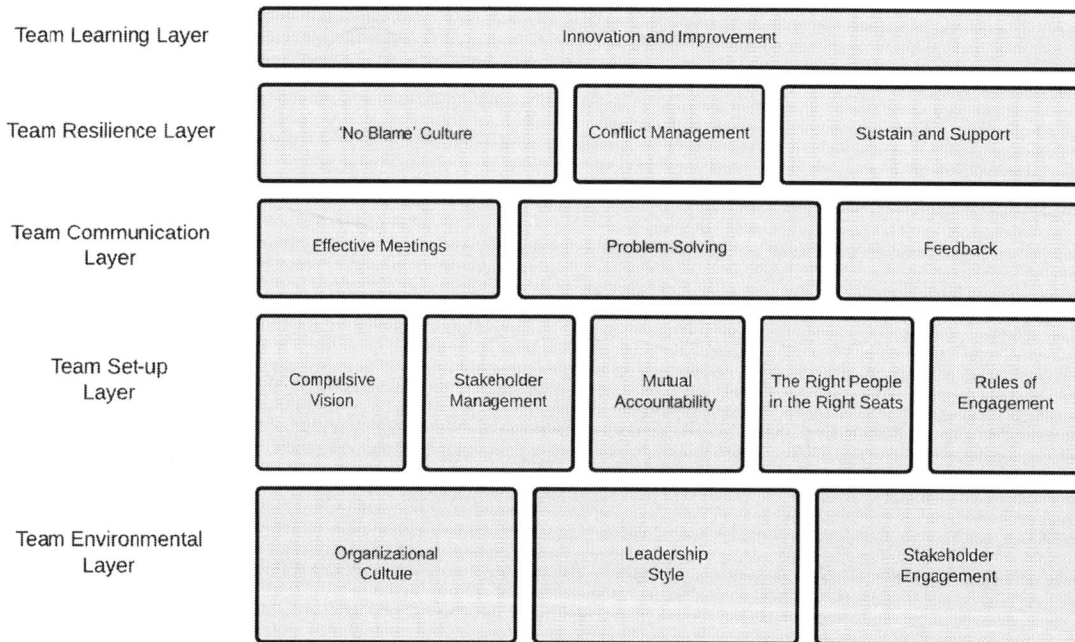

Team Learning Layer	Innovation and Improvement				
Team Resilience Layer	'No Blame' Culture	Conflict Management		Sustain and Support	
Team Communication Layer	Effective Meetings	Problem-Solving		Feedback	
Team Set-up Layer	Compulsive Vision	Stakeholder Management	Mutual Accountability	The Right People in the Right Seats	Rules of Engagement
Team Environmental Layer	Organizational Culture	Leadership Style		Stakeholder Engagement	

Figure 1 – The foundation layers of an effective team

Figure 1 identifies many of the features of an effective team. The people engagement processes can be grouped into metaphorical blocks which can then be used to build the team's commitment and accountability. These blocks form the foundation stones upon which strong teamwork is built. Like the foundations of a building, they are out of sight and therefore invisible to the uneducated eye. We know that it may be possible to assemble a wooden shed upon some hardened ground, but if we want to build something bigger that needs to survive unstable ground conditions then good foundations are essential.

Layer	Function
Environment	Early assessment of a range of systemic factors enabling a leader to understand the influences imposed on the team by the cultural and social conditions in which the team will operate.
Set-up	Setting up the team to establish the desired behavioural norms. Includes the activities and processes that have been found to be critical in building motivation, stability and interdependence.
Communication	Sets the mechanisms for the effective interaction between team members and with those in the team's periphery.
Resilience	Activities that will support and sustain the team through periods of difficulty. Builds trust within the team and sets up the protocols needed to withstand the pressures of unplanned and adverse changes.
Learning and improvement	Developing the habit of periodically reviewing what the team has recently achieved, what has worked well, and what can be improved in the next iteration.

Table 1 – The foundation layers of the team building process

The construction analogy is valid insofar as these foundations are best put in place before a team begins to focus on getting things done. In the same way that one can always go back and underpin a failing structure, it is possible to carry out remedial work on a dysfunctional team. Such work, however, tends to be messy, disruptive and can often 'annoy the neighbours'. It is therefore worth taking time to assemble the appropriate structures at the team's inception. As illustrated in table 1, the layers represent the different phases of a team's progression. They are, to a certain extent, sequential in that good practice involves putting the right layers in place at the right time. The tools in this book therefore are set out to align with this structure. The structure is explained in more detail in the next chapter. This does not mean you necessarily always have to start with a new team for the toolkit to be of use. As you will see when you look through the different tools, each will work as a stand-alone exercise. The point of this structure is to encourage you to recognize how the different tools will work at different stages of the team's life cycle.

REAL TEAMS NOT WORKGROUPS

Without trying to complicate the discussion by going into the technical detail, it is worth recognizing the practical difference between a real team and a workgroup. We often casually use the word *team* to include any group of people who happen to report to the same manager. If, however, the day-to-day work of the group is not generally dependent upon the success of others in that group then, from an academic perspective, this is simply a *workgroup*. It is easy to get lost in the semantics of nomenclature but, for the purposes of this toolkit, the definition is important. There are many possible ways to define what constitutes a real team. My personal preference comes from Katzenbach and Smith (1993) who define a team as 'a small number of people with complimentary skills who are committed to a common purpose, performance goals, and an approach for which they hold themselves mutually accountable'.

There is a lot of content in this single sentence. The key words form a useful checklist as set out in the table below.

Key words	Implication
Small number	Between five and nine members
Complimentary skills	Distinct skills needed to complete the task
Commitment	Emotional rather than notional
Common purpose	Everyone focused on the same thing
Performance goals	An agreed outcome
An approach	One agreed system
Mutually accountable	If one of us fails, we all fail

Table 2 – Real team checklist

As you work your way down this table, you can start to see why genuine teams are less common than we think. Real teamwork is rarely accidental. These components are often difficult to establish and maintain. The distinction between a notional team and a real team is therefore important. The coaching and leadership needs of a collection of individuals who must achieve a challenging goal are very different to a group that simply needs to complete a series of tasks set for them by their supervisor.

I frequently hear managers talking about creating 'high performing teams' with little sense as to what it really means and the effort required to get there. This is an overused phrase that has become detached from its original definition. It is almost a slogan whose meaning is frequently used to imply that all teams should somehow or other be able to deliver exceptional results or risk being dismissed as a failure. High performing teams tend to emerge, rather than be planned, and will usually disperse once the goal or objective has been reached.

The word *performance* has itself become a piece of management jargon. In the context of an individual or team, the dictionary definition of the word is simply 'an action'. In management speak it has come to imply a level of achievement. A more accurate and perhaps more meaningful word is *effective* which is defined as 'successful in producing the desired or intended result'. Teams may not often be able to achieve the rarefied heights of being regarded as *high performing*, but it is a much more realistic aspiration in any organization that the team should be regarded as working effectively. A far better ambition is to be part of a highly effective team, in that it is both readily achievable and sustainable provided both the leader and the team are prepared to put in the work.

WHAT KIND OF TEAM DO YOU NEED?

This is an important question. As mentioned above, creating a genuine team is hard work. It takes time, energy and a lot of thought. The resources required are not always easily available, particularly when you are working under pressure. Building a *real team* may be impractical and unnecessary. Creating a collaborative, energized group is often a highly satisfying process, but it may not be essential to the delivery of your team's objective. There are many situations where *real teams* are less important. Some examples include:

- Organizations dealing with processing of goods or information, where the inputs and outputs are largely predictable and there is little variation.
- Small organizations where the leader/manager can handle the majority of external interfaces and directs her assistants on the specific tasks needed to fulfil her objectives.
- Organizations with fixed hierarchical structures and strong cultural norms around communication, which exist in stable environments not subject to external economic, social or political pressures.
- Steering committees (which could include the Management Board) whose role is to find consensus amongst a group of individuals representing their own department or workgroup.

As a general rule, if you believe you can maintain genuine control of your internal environment and external conditions are stable, then the short-term transactional arrangements of a *workgroup* will probably be sufficient. There are many examples of organizations where process and procedure are strongly embedded, establishing a degree of stability and consistency. The culture of conformity that has emerged in these organizations works well, up to the point that the external environment changes.

As the world shifts, however, the foundations upon which conformity is built will start to become less stable. When organizations need to work out how to adapt to the disruptive forces of change, that is when we need *real teams*. So consider what kind of team you would like and then think again about the team that you are actually going to need.

Large complex projects need to engage a range of skills and experience to design and deliver the desired outcome. Few teams have the luxury of a prolonged selection process to choose the perfect profile. Most members are chosen on their perceived ability and the extent to which it is felt they will fit. Beware of creating teams that are too homogenous, i.e. made up of people just like you. Whilst such teams have been shown to gel quickly, they usually lack the creative edge needed to overcome difficult problems. Alternatively everyone is so action-oriented that the individuals ultimately fall into conflict.

PICKING THE RIGHT TOOLS FOR THE JOB

Building the norms you need requires choosing the right tools for the job. Some tools should be standard to every team's early development. Understanding where complexity is likely to be an issue, particularly with external stakeholders, will encourage every member to start looking beyond their own specific area of expertise and see the challenge as a whole (**Tool 1**). Assessing the project environment (**Tool 2**) is an explicit mechanism that ensures the team know from the start what they are likely to be up against.

There are some standard norms that need to be discussed and established early on. Meetings should have clear rules around timekeeping, use of mobile phones during meetings and the recording of agreed actions. Whilst these rules should ultimately be non-negotiable you will find that compliance is much stronger if the team feels they have created the rules rather than having them imposed (**Tool 13**). The tools that shape communication such as the use of collaborative language (**Tool 22**) and allowing everyone to have a voice (**Tool 24**) are good examples of the direct use of mechanisms to establish positive behaviours that may be specific to your team. These tools are explicit and the outcome of any discussion should be recorded in writing and the team held to account if they do not comply.

There are other rules that establish less comfortable norms depending upon the team's mission. If excellence/best in class is going to be required to achieve a tough goal, how are you going to go about it? For example, do you need the team to be challenging each other, pushing the best ideas to the top (**Tool 34**)? This can be quite disruptive to group process, but if you aspire to excellence then this is what will be needed. Similarly, if the team is working through a complex series of tasks, its effectiveness will significantly improve if it willingly seeks feedback both from within the team and from its stakeholders. The team therefore need to be open to criticism and to use feedback to learn and then adapt (**Tools 14 and 42**).

Other norms are shaped more subtly. Tools for establishing a compulsive vision (**Tool 10** – 'The Big "Why"') and 'Building a future story' (**Tool 15**) do not place any rules on the team, but instead nudge the team to focus on what they have in common, irrespective of their different personal and professional backgrounds. The development of trust has repeatedly been shown to be fundamental to the development of a cohesive unit. The more time team members take to understand each other, the stronger the bonds that will hold them together. So whilst mutual understanding is a powerful norm, you cannot create a rule or process that will force it to happen. Instead you must rely on the tools that will help build mutual comprehension. There is great value to be had from encouraging a team to reveal their fears and vulnerabilities. Studies consistently show that once team members start to empathize with each other at a deeper level, they bond more closely and really start to become mutually accountable. Exercises such as 'How to motivate or annoy me' (**Tool 16**) are a great start, but any of the tools that encourage the team to explain both what they think and what they feel will help strengthen the team.

The book also includes some remedial tools to help the team regain its balance. These are particularly useful on long projects where fatigue can set in and inter-personal conflict starts to affect the team dynamic. Tools such as 'Press reset' (**Tool 32**) and 'Establishing a "no blame" culture' (**Tool 19**) help the team look at itself as an entity and try to regain some perspective. Maintaining the resilience of a team has generally been neglected in both the academic literature and in management best practice. Stoicism and mental toughness are admirable qualities but, as a number of recent studies have shown, every individual has a breaking point. Strong teams sustain their members through difficult times and so the resilience tools provide a useful set of exercises to roll out when everyone is starting to feel the pressure.

You now have in your hands some of the key tools with which to shape and build the dynamics of your team. To become a master craftsman, however, takes time and practice. Influencing behavioural norms requires a different approach to leadership, based around a coaching philosophy. This is covered in the next chapter.

CHAPTER 3

THE EMERGENCE OF THE TEAM COACH

The concept of applying coaching techniques to improve the performance of a work-based team is rapidly gaining traction. At a time when one-to-one executive coaching is becoming a mainstream activity more leaders are also starting to pay attention to the effectiveness of their teams.

Writing in 2017, it is possible to see the coaching industry begin to mature. Business schools and specialist colleges are retraining thousands of men and women seeking a career change to become certified coaches. In the past, coaching has been seen as an expensive and therefore exclusive resource restricted to the executive level. As its value has become recognized, one–to-one coaching is increasingly being developed as an 'in-house' capability where managers are encouraged to develop the soft skills associated with coaching as a mechanism to develop their direct reports.

As more organizations realize the limitations of the command and control paradigm, there is a growing recognition that attention needs to move beyond the individual and focus on the ability of the team. The unit of productivity in any large organization is the team not the individual, and yet Western culture tends to focus on the success and failure of the individual rather than the group or tribe. In business, success tends to be attributed to individual leaders with little credit given to the teams who actually delivered the outcome. Similarly when something goes wrong someone must be seen to have been responsible even though the failure must have emanated from all the people tasked with achieving the goal or deadline.

As we will go on to discuss in this chapter, leadership is critically important. However, the point I would stress here is that informed organizations and smart leaders are explicitly aware it is teams that account for sustainable and repetitive success. Having great individuals in your team makes a difference but it is the way in which everyone works together that ultimately makes the difference between the good, the bad and the ugly.

Team coaching in sporting activities is a well-established and understood role. Many sporting bodies have established training and qualification levels to develop an individual's capability to coach a team. In the world of work team coaching is much less well known. There are, however, many individual practitioners who have each developed their own processes for working with teams that could be regarded as a form of team coaching. These pioneers had little information upon which to develop their practice. They have simply built up their methodologies on instinct and experience. It is nevertheless fascinating to listen to their stories, and see how different managers, leaders and coaches have developed their own team coaching processes that broadly align around a similar core set of principles. In the last decade, practitioners and academics such as Peter Hawkins and David Clutterbuck began to pull the various strands of research into team performance and group dynamics into a structure that is slowly developing into a more standardized methodology. The use of team coaching is nevertheless in its infancy. The concepts and processes intrinsic to team coaching are still largely being developed by enthusiasts and are yet to become mainstream components of organizational activity. This is, however, likely to change over the next few years as more project managers and team leaders recognize the value in paying attention to team process.

It is important to recognize that team coaching is more than facilitation. Whilst many coaches and leadership consultants may claim to have been working with teams for many years, their work is often limited to sporadic interventions such as the facilitation of away days or mediation of teams in distress. Team coaching in its purer form is a much more involved activity. It requires a different perspective, where one is primarily concerned with the team as an entity, rather than as a set of individuals. The focus for the team coach is the outcome that underpins the team's reason to exist, and how it achieves that goal successfully. It is tempting to dive into the semantics of definitions to illustrate how different authors have tried to explain what team coaching actually involves. However, this is not intended to be an academic book and so I will limit the discussion to a definition I have used in the past to establish the range of activity in coaching teams engaged in projects or other discrete activities which have a clear goal and outcome.

Project team coaching is the application of a series of interventions that enable a project team to develop and implement the collaborative behaviours required to deliver the desired outcomes of the stakeholders, to the performance standards that the team expect of themselves (Llewellyn, 2015).

The salient points in this definition are:

- the coaching role is enabling rather than directing
- the key to real teamwork is collaboration
- the coach's role is focused on the desired project outcomes, not on the team as individuals
- the team decide what their performance standards should be, and
- the role can be part of, or distinct from, the role of project leadership.

I have chosen to focus this book on teams involved in projects or cross-functional initiatives. This does not mean the tools and techniques are not applicable to standing work teams or executive teams, as many of the ideas are useful for anyone working to improve the dynamics of a group. My choice is based on the observation that so many people spend their working lives involved to a greater or lesser extent in projects. Projects need teams, and the larger the project the more support is required to manage the complexity. In the context of coaching, an intervention is an action designed to encourage an individual, or a group, to pause and consider their approach to a problem and assess the alternatives. In most cases, coaching interventions are in the form of questions.

WHAT TYPE OF TEAM COACH ARE YOU?

The majority of management books are written as instruction manuals aimed at the CEO and other senior decision makers. This book is not written for the CEO. It is for the people who actually deliver the organization's output. As discussed in the introduction, this book is written for three potentially distinct audiences.

1. A leader of a cross-functional team assembled from internal resources within an organization tasked with delivering some form of initiative or project outcome.

2. A project manager leading a team of experts assembled from a variety of external consultants and contractors.

3. A coach commissioned to support an internal or external team in creating and then maintaining the processes and systems needed to establish an effectively functioning team.

It is of course quite possible to be involved in a hybrid of any of these situations but for the purpose of this chapter I will treat them as contrasting scenarios. There are clear merits in being able to address issues specific to the concerns of a sector or professional group. The challenges of working with groups of human beings are nevertheless broadly similar whatever your area of focus. As we will see, techniques for motivating people, gaining commitment and providing mutual support are largely similar. What changes is the context of each situation.

The challenges each of the above three roles face is likely to be quite specific to their task. A project manager trying to lead a team of external consultants will need a different approach to a leader of a cross-functional team wrestling with the internal politics of a large organization. Before we press on to the detail of the tools and techniques, it is therefore worth looking at the concept of how team coaching might apply to each of the three categories.

FROM TEAM LEADER TO TEAM COACH

As discussed in the previous chapter, middle managers working in command and control cultures face a difficult challenge in building a committed and engaged workforce. Looking to the future, however, it is easy to see a different environment where management success comes from the ability to lead energized teams. Leadership in the 21st century is a complicated role. You need to operate in conditions where the ground rules are continually uncertain. Irrespective of your position in the organization you must consistently maintain your relationships with your stakeholders, managers and subordinates. To survive and thrive as a team leader in the 21st century, it is also worth paying some attention to your team's sub-culture. Culture dominates how people behave and whilst one cannot ignore the overarching culture of an organization every part of a large entity develops their own sub-culture.

Culture is fundamentally about 'how we do things around here'. It is a set of tacit or unspoken rules that develop over time. Culture influences how relationships in a team are expected to play out, setting the rules on what is discussed and what is not. In 'steady state', when the environment is calm, most team members learn how to work around the limitations of their culture without difficulty. It is when a team comes under pressure that a successful culture reveals itself.

Teams learn their behaviours from various sources. Some behaviours are imported from other teams but most of the influences will come from the leader. Cultural attributes found in successful teams include:

- strong core values that have meaning for the team
- a clear purpose and vision as to why the team exists
- a high degree of autonomy as to how work is accomplished
- a desire to continually improve
- a positive attitude to change and quick to adapt to new circumstances, and
- transparency in all of the team's internal and external interactions.

These attributes do not usually develop by themselves. They require someone to initiate and reinforce them so they become habitual.

Bernard Bass (1990) introduced the term 'transformational leadership' to describe an alternative approach to the traditional top-down 'transactional' managerial mindset. He was seeking to articulate a distinct style whereby the leader becomes less focused on the completion of organizational process and seeks instead to make greater use of the resources available to the team. Transformational leadership is therefore characterized by a strong focus around people and how to foster an environment where the team take greater ownership of the collective goals and objectives. Transformational leadership style is less focused on control and more absorbed with helping the team be successful by nurturing individual talent and removing obstacles that slow the team's progress.

Originally coined by Robert Greenleaf (1970), the term 'servant leadership' has increasingly gained acceptance in management theory around leadership. The primary concept is that the purpose of the leader is to serve the team rather than the team serve the leader. This idea sits uncomfortably in a hierarchical culture, and yet it is a useful way of thinking about team coaching as an alternative approach to leadership. As servant leader your role is primarily as an enabler, providing guidance and support rather than instruction. Whether this makes sense to you will depend on how you view your relationship with your team. Is the role of individuals in your team to implement your directions, or do you believe in encouraging greater autonomy of individual decision-making?

There are many potential paths one might take to develop a transformational or servant leadership style, but one of the simplest routes is to adopt a team coaching mindset. In the context of a cross-functional workgroup this style makes more sense, as trying to *control* individuals from other departments where you do not have line management authority is likely to be a futile task. If people outside of your line management responsibility do not like your instructions, it is always easy to find a way to disengage from your project. Far better to focus on those activities that will draw people into your project and create a team culture where they are happy to contribute additional discretionary effort to build a successful outcome.

FROM PROJECT MANAGER TO TEAM COACH

The project management profession can be seen to have been in a state of continuous development over the last 40 years. A role that started with coordination and planning has developed into a much broader skill set. Project managers are typically generous in sharing their knowledge and an extensive range of best practice systems process and certified qualifications have been embedded internationally. The demand for the project manager is predicted to continue to grow as the world continues to adapt to social, technological and political disruption. The challenge, however, is that the project managers who are most in demand will need to have a much broader skill set.

Over the past five years there has been an increasing level of interest in the adoption of Agile Project Management (APM) (Beck *et al.*, 2001), both as a technical skill set and as a philosophical approach to the delivery of projects. A movement that started in the software industry is slowly extending to the wider project management community. There are many technical aspects to the APM process which are beyond the scope of this book. There are, however, some critical shifts that are very relevant to the concept of team coaching.

Historically, a project manager emerged from some form of technical profession or sector, be it technology, engineering, construction etc. Most project managers continue to have a high level of understanding around the technical challenges arising in their projects. This attribute is highly useful in complicated projects where the primary challenge is coordination of the programme. It is less valuable when the project shifts from complicated to complex and must move quickly from iteration to iteration continually adjusting to stakeholder feedback (see **Technique 7** – 'Adopt an "Agile" mindset').

APM is just one example of the broader trend in the project management profession. An increasing number of commentators believe project managers can no longer rely solely on their organizational skills to remain employable. Advances in technology and commoditization are making much of the PM process either obsolete or easily outsourced. In the midst of uncertainty, however, someone needs to be seen to be holding a degree of control as to how the project can progress. Logically this is the project manager, and they are the only one who, in theory at least, has access to most of the information. The role of PM therefore shifts from ringmaster to guide, providing the direction of travel whist members of the team establish the route. The value that clients are going to be seeking in the future is more likely to be in the ability to help manage complexity, drive change and stimulate innovation.

These outcomes require the skills needed to manage teams in a different way. Lyssa Adkins (2010) identifies some of the changes in approach that take place as the PM moves from primary controller to team coach. I have adapted her observations in table 3.

These shifts in approach may sit uncomfortably with many experienced project managers who have become used to the traditional directive approach. The changes can, however, be made over time as you experiment with the 'Agile' approach and test out the new mindset. Adkins

(2010) describes the move from project manager to team coach as a journey with many twists and turns along the way. Arriving at the destination is, however, worth the effort.

A move away from	A move towards
Coordinating individuals	Helping the team learn to collaborate
Subject matter expert	Being a facilitator for the team
A focus on specific outcomes	An overriding interest in the overall performance
Knowing the answer	Asking the team for the answer
Directing	Encouraging the team to find their own way
Driving	Guiding
Fixing problems	Taking problems to the team

Table 3 – A changing approach to project management

FROM EXECUTIVE COACH TO TEAM COACH

The third segment of potential team coaches are individuals who have trained to coach on a one-to-one basis and find themselves being asked to work with teams. The position here is not as leader, but as support to the team. It is easy to envisage a future where coaches increasingly spend some, or all, of their time working with teams rather than individuals. This is partly because the number of projects requiring cohesive teams is going to increase. The practice of team coaching will also continue to mature. As organizations and project leaders experience the benefit of team coaching support, they are more likely to seek it out for every project in their portfolio.

The most common progression from coach to team coach is in response to a request from a client with whom the coach is working. It is quite common for an executive coach to be asked to help work with the senior team or to run an off-site event. For many coaches, this is also the limit of their experience in working with teams. Coaching a group of individuals requires a number of critical shifts in thinking. The most important adjustment is to recognize why you are there. Team coaching is not about providing individual development support for a number of people who happen to be on the same team. That is merely a matter of serial coaching.

Coaching a team primarily requires helping them achieve their *collective* purpose. Your mindset as a team coach needs to pull back from the individual and to think about the team as a single entity. To be of any value to the team your support must be focused on helping them move towards their goal, providing those interventions that technical teams lack either in terms of expertise or simply because they do not have the time.

The primary area of value provided by an external team coach is to help the team develop the behavioural norms that are going to be needed for the team to function effectively as a collaborative unit. Technical people have an almost irresistible urge to leap straight into task progression and the first steps of project delivery. The role of the coach is to encourage the team to think about the challenges ahead and how they will deal with them (see **Technique 3** – 'Slow down to speed up').

Many of the coaching skills learned in one-to-one coaching are relevant to working with teams. The ability to recognize the underlying dynamics of the group, to ask insightful questions and to really listen to the responses are part of the primary skills set. The challenge is to be able to raise your awareness so you are able to see and hear all of the information coming from their interactions with you but more importantly from each other.

Tuning into body language, inter-personal relationships and organizational history can help you see what is going on beneath the surface. The role is not, however, just about the relationships inside the team. The team coach should be able to think systemically, understanding the influences that sit outside the team which will also affect their behaviour. Since most of a team coach's work is with the team as a group, strong facilitation skills are also essential.

A word of caution. Individuals who are drawn to team coaching are typically comfortable standing at the front of the room and controlling the agenda. The external team coach must be clear that his or her role is to provide support to the team but not to usurp the role of the leader. There is a common and recurring problem where the enthusiasm and alternative thinking introduced by the external facilitator impress the team to the extent they take on the status of temporary team leader. This is not helpful to anyone in that, once the team coach leaves the room, behaviours and thinking revert to their previous levels. The team coach must therefore work closely with the team leader and ensure the role is to support rather than become a quasi component of the technical delivery.

A MODEL OF TEAM COACHING FOR COACHING PROJECT TEAMS

If you wish to build a team that must succeed in uncertain conditions it is worth understanding some of the fundamentals of how a group evolves into a team. It is, to a certain extent, a scientific process in that studies of effective teams throw out the same critical steps that need to be in place. On the other hand there is also an art to team development, partly because every new team will be unique, both in the personalities who make up the group, and how they relate to each other. Creating, developing and nurturing a team requires attention be paid to two key elements: i. Task delivery – how the team will go about delivering their work; and ii. Team process – how the individuals will work together as a cohesive unit.

Task delivery revolves around the planning, organization of resources and dealing with the technical challenges required to achieve the objective. Team process is concerned with how the team will actually work together. Team coaching is primarily concerned with team process, but always in the context of the need to achieve the outcome through effective task completion.

The tools in this book are arranged around a model for coaching project teams as set out in the figure 2. The model is derived from a range of studies on team performance, group dynamics and project efficiency. Whilst there are a range of different models around which one can learn to coach a team, projects offer their own particular challenges in setting and maintaining the collaborative behaviours needed to solve complex problems.

Models are useful in providing a simplified explanation or perspective of a potentially complicated issue. They are also helpful in creating an overview into which different scenarios might apply. All models lack context and so there are limitations as to how reliable they can be in covering every eventuality. The reader must consequently take them for what they are, an abstract concept which provides an indication of the right direction of travel, but does not necessarily affect external reality.

The model is intended to provide a framework within which the different tools can be used. To a certain extent the model is sequential in that some activities need to take place early in the project cycle to set the right behavioural norms. Other consolidating activities then follow. In the real world, however, complex projects are not so tidy in their structure or programme. Projects start and then stall for a while. People join and leave at unplanned intervals and the external environment is constantly shifting. The model should therefore be regarded as a guide, rather than a set of rules.

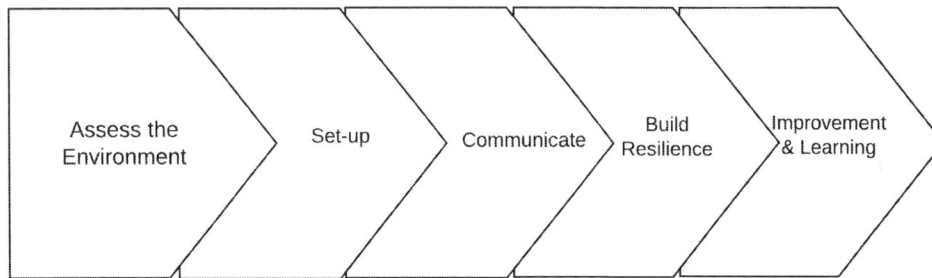

```
Assess the          Set-up      Communicate    Build       Improvement
Environment                                    Resilience   & Learning
```

Figure 2 – Team coaching model

The team coaching model works around five key stages.

ASSESS THE SYSTEMIC ENVIRONMENT

This first stage is about building a realistic awareness of the extent of the challenge the team is taking on, so they are going into the project with their eyes wide open. The process requires a dispassionate view of organizational and environmental limitations that are going to affect the way the team functions. Human beings are notoriously over-optimistic when assessing risk on a project or initiative they want to proceed. Too many projects fail because assumptions were made at the start that were never realistically going to materialize.

As illustrated in **Tools 2 and 3**, it is therefore useful to go through a sequence of questions to test what is driving the project, whether the stakeholder's expectations are realistic, and the sponsor is fully committed to your success. This is the time to check the budget is realistic, the programme is deliverable and the resources needed are going to be available. These are forces that are out of the team's immediate control, but not beyond its influence. If conditions appear to be sub-optimal at the beginning, they pose a real risk to the team's ultimate ability to perform. Another element of this stage therefore involves the team leader opening a dialogue with the sponsor and stakeholders to ensure everyone is aware of the risks, and where necessary steps are taken to improve the environmental conditions. This is a discussion to have before the project picks up momentum. Once activity gets underway any discussion on problems caused by a lack of planning are likely to come across as excuses. Engaging with the other parties at an early stage gives you the ability to have an assertive conversation where you can ask influential questions and assert your position without having to resort to confrontation.

SET-UP AND INITIATION

The research on team performance consistently identifies five steps that have been found to be critical to establishing positive behavioural norms. Many people are familiar with the Forming, Storming, Norming and Performing model of team development put forward by Bruce Tuckman (1965). This is the stage where as team leader or team coach you are able to shape the team's behaviours as the team works though the forming and storming stages. The five elements are:

- establish a clear and compulsive vision around which the team can align
- clarify the key stakeholder relationships and agree a plan to engage and communicate with them
- ensure you have the right people on the team, with the right skills and the right attitude
- agree the ground rules as to how the team members will behave, both when they meet together and when they connect outside the meeting to deliver the team's objective, and

- gain agreement for individual and collective accountability.

This stage is not optional. The work is usually achieved in a project initiation workshop which should ideally be held over a two-day period to allow the team to start to get to know each other. Few complex projects succeed if the behavioural set-up is omitted. Despite the evidence, it is surprising how many teams ignore this stage and leap into the task execution, only to find to their cost that poor team behaviours quickly slow their progress.

ENABLE EXECUTION BY LEARNING TO COMMUNICATE

So far so good, now comes the difficult part. All of the good intentions established in the set-up workshop need to turn into action. I have come across many teams who invest quality time in a successful workshop, and then immediately revert to the transactional processes of task completion. Someone needs to take responsibility for the implementation of the implementation plan and to ensure the agreed behavioural norms are established and embedded. Where teams lack the expertise, it is the role of the team coach to pick up this important responsibility. The execution phase also requires the coach to maintain an overview of the processes, routines and activities that maintain clear communication, encourage dialogue and ensure clarity of understanding.

BUILDING RESILIENCE

The next element of the model is to prepare for those periods in a project when the team comes under collective pressure to perform. There are a variety of activities that come under the heading of team resilience, a number of which are set out in the toolkit. Examples include the mechanics and protocols for managing relationship conflict, monitoring stress and learning to improve the team's ability to handle bad news without defaulting to a blame culture. Your objective as team coach, however, is to start to build resilience into the team before the pressure hits, so that the team collectively learn how to adjust to problems such as a shortage of resources, impending deadlines and changes in scope. Strong teams learn to thrive under pressure and, in some sectors, resilience can be seen as a source of competitive advantage.

EMBED LEARNING

Studies show that great teams pay attention to continuous improvement. This requires taking time out of the delivery process at regular intervals to examine how they have been working and agree ways of improving. This may sound straightforward, but most teams lack both the mindset and the structure to practise iterative learning. The team coaching role therefore includes helping the team develop the mechanisms by which they can review, reflect, plan and then put into action better ways of delivering the outcome.

SUMMARY

Using coaching tools and techniques can be a challenging process. It takes patience, which can be difficult when external pressures exert a level of urgency to demonstrate fast results. Building great teams requires the development of some harder to learn 'soft skills'. You must make an investment in the process of learning, experimenting with and adapting the different techniques to suit your personal style. The payoff is, however, potentially huge, not just in terms of team performance and productivity, but also in personal satisfaction as you watch your team grow and succeed beyond their own individual expectations.

SECTION TWO

Team Coaching Techniques

In the following section you will find 10 techniques that will help you apply the tools set out in Section Three more effectively.

Technique 1	Systemic thinking and the spheres of influence
Technique 2	Facilitating a thinking environment
Technique 3	Slow down to speed up
Technique 4	Curious enquiry
Technique 5	Influential questions
Technique 6	Listening for clues
Technique 7	Adopt an 'Agile' mindset
Technique 8	Using case stories
Technique 9	The importance of visual information
Technique 10	Developing your maturity in complexity

A technique is defined 'as a way of doing something'. A good technique makes the action easier or more elegant. It is a learned activity which can be developed over time. Put a collection of techniques together and you start to develop a work philosophy.

The techniques set out in the following pages explain some of the core processes that sit at the heart of coaching a team, particularly when working with a project team. They represent a way of thinking about how you approach each different team scenario you are faced with. Some of the techniques require a shift in perspective, whilst others are quite practical.

Learning to apply them consistently will help you develop your confidence as a coach and a leader. As you read through this section, think about the extent to which you currently work this way and how you might explore and experiment with each concept to improve your skills.

SYSTEMIC THINKING AND THE SPHERES OF INFLUENCE

WHAT IS SYSTEMIC THINKING?

Systemic thinking is a mechanism for looking at a problem or issue from a number of different perspectives. Rather than reacting to an event by jumping to an immediate conclusion based on your perception of cause and effect, systemic thinking encourages you to understand the impact that different systems will have on a situation or event. The process requires the team coach to slow down and ask a broader series of questions.

WHY IS IT USEFUL?

A systemic approach can be particularly useful in understanding the apparently complex patterns of behaviour that can be observed in people working in groups or teams. Understanding these forces improves the chances that a solution can be found to potential problems by addressing the root cause of the problem, not just symptoms.

THE THEORY

Human beings rarely operate in isolation, but instead work as part of a system (or variety of systems). Our behaviour is strongly influenced by each of the systems we become a part of. A system is made up of a number of interconnected activities that are continuously adapted by the people in the system as they react to events outside of the system.

Systemic thinking is sometimes described as a way of seeing the structures that underlie complex situations. An event may appear to have been caused by a particular sequence of actions but, in reality, the cause extends beyond the initial evidence. Our first reaction to most problems tends to be instinctive and emotional. Our mental processes do not therefore seek all of the information that would be required to understand the full breadth of the issue. Systems theory prompts you to look at all of the other factors that will have an influence on the system in which the event occurred.

IN PRACTICE

So how can you actually apply systemic thinking in the context of managing complex behaviours within a team? The starting point is to recognize the need to look beyond the obvious, and consider the full range of factors that may have an influence on the problem or issue. This action requires you to try and ignore your instinctive response and take the time to reflect on what has happened, and what is currently happening, in the systems. In essence, you need to ask a different set of questions. This is an exercise that you can do by yourself, but it also works effectively if you involve other members of your team.

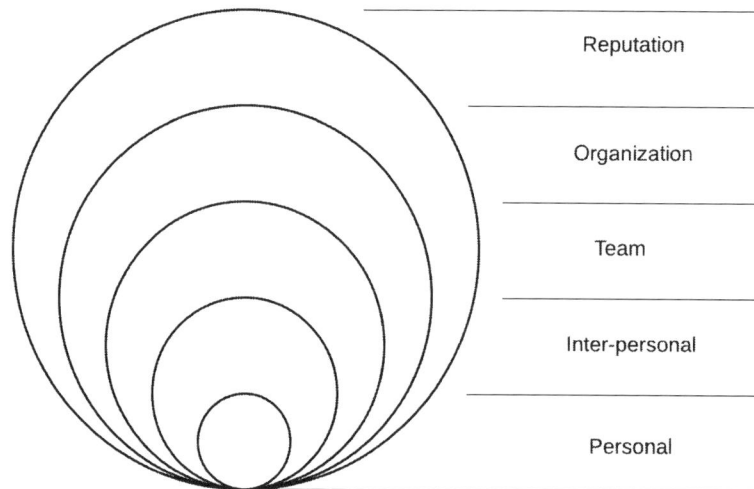

Figure 3 – The spheres of influence

My friends, Will Karlsen and Adrian Wheeler, have come up with a visual graphic that helps illustrate the concept of what they have termed the 'spheres of influence' as illustrated in figure 3. Each sphere represents a different aspect of human interaction with an organization either at a personal, inter-personal or team level. The organization also exists within a wider sphere in which it must interact with its staff and its stakeholders. In trying to understand why an individual or even a team is behaving in a particular way, the systemic approach prompts you to consider the influence that all five spheres may be having on the situation.

The underlying theory is that most complex situations need to be looked at through the lens of all five of the spheres. Each lens calls for a different perspective enabling the viewer to see the issue from different sides, providing a richer source of data with which to decide a course of action. It is a mechanism to prompt the secondary questions that may help reveal deeper issues. For the purposes of illustration, let us pick an example of a disagreement between the team and an influential stakeholder, who we will call Susan. She has upset the team by making comments that are perceived to lack respect for the work the team is doing. Your instinctive reaction is to be defensive of your colleagues and dismiss Susan as 'an idiot' (or some other euphemism). The team now regard this person as an opponent and start to blame her for creating perceived barriers to their progress. The problem, however, is by assuming her intentions you limit your options in trying to rebuild a positive relationship. A systemic approach prompts you to ask a series of additional questions before you reach a conclusion.

The initial conversation has been through the *Inter-personal* sphere, so the systemic process requires that first you recognize your own emotional reaction and that you try to take a dispassionate view of the situation through the other lenses. The *Personal* sphere is now used to try and understand the psychological drivers of the stakeholder or the project sponsor. Based on what you know of her, what drives her behaviours? Does she appear to be motivated by an orientation towards people, process or performance? Do you think she is a strategic thinker or does she appear to like to get into the detail? Since you cannot read her mind, all you can do is look for clues that might give you a better understanding of her apparent attitude. The reverse view through the *Personal* sphere may also be relevant. Do you understand your own drivers and emotional reactions? What were your early interactions with Susan and do they have an impact on how you regard her? Knowing your own preferences, motivations and biases is always useful as they will subconsciously shape your opinions and attitudes.

You now have both the personal and inter-personal perspectives. The next step is to pull back and look through the lens of the team. What are the interactions between the stakeholder and the team as a collective unit? Does the sponsor really understand the team's mission and the challenges it must overcome? Is the team looking for a scapegoat upon which to load the frustrations which may be arising from other areas of the project? So how should the team as an entity re-engage with the stakeholder to ensure her future support?

Re-engagement, however, may not be sufficient. It may well be the case that Susan's criticism was a result of pressures affecting the wider organization of which you were unaware. So what are the cultural and political forces that may be affecting people outside of the team? Erratic behaviours often start to make sense when you look at a situation through the *Organizational* lens.

The final perspective comes by looking through the *Reputational* lens. This requires considering the forces that are affecting the organization from the outside world. Pressure comes from those external bodies or individuals who have a direct or indirect effect on decision-making, such as customers, shareholders or tax payers. In the modern world, how an organization is perceived can be critically important. Reputation can affect whether customers stay loyal, whether financial markets will provide funding, and whether an institution can be trusted to act with integrity. When external events start to create uncertainty and ambiguity, high level decision-making can often be slightly bewildering.

This process of asking questions through different perspectives is a very useful technique for providing a much richer level of information through which to understand what is really going on. Practised over time it helps you quickly look for data that lies beneath the surface and ask questions that will help the team not only avoid jumping to inaccurate conclusions but help them find better answers to difficult situations.

FACILITATING A THINKING ENVIRONMENT

WHAT IS A THINKING ENVIRONMENT?

The technique of continually creating the right conditions to encourage the team to think both individually and collectively. It is a facilitation role.

WHY IS IT USEFUL?

In urgent and pressurized situations humans often lose the ability to think clearly and focus on routine process. One of your roles as team coach is to create the conditions that encourage everyone on the team to think around an issue and then collectively decide how to move forward.

THE THEORY

Nancy Kline sets out a number of conditions for creating a 'thinking environment' (Kline, 1999). She picks out some core coaching attributes such as paying attention, asking incisive questions and the equal treatment of each person as a 'thinking peer'. Her primary message is that everyone has the capability to think more clearly once the clutter of day-to-day activity has been parked to one side. Your role as team coach is to facilitate that process.

The word facilitate can be defined as the action of making a process easier. An important part of the role of team coach is to facilitate the team's ability to find answers to problems by helping them think. This might seem a slightly ridiculous suggestion when you are working with a team of bright, capable individuals but thinking as a group requires someone to manage the thinking sequence so that everyone is momentarily absorbed on the same issue. Facilitation is therefore an important team coaching skill where you are creating the best possible environment to encourage the team to think.

The concept of a thinking environment works at a number of levels. Attention must be paid to every factor that will impact on the team's creative ability to engage with a problem. This will include issues such as the physical setting, relevance of the agenda and, of course, the behavioural dynamics of the group.

Effective facilitation requires more than the administration of a meeting or workshop. Helping the team to think also requires the right questions to be posed at the right time. The coaching skill is to find the balance of involvement in the discussion where you are seen to be keeping a conversation moving without dominating the thinking of others.

The thinking environment works in different ways but predominantly requires the team to engage with each other around the matter under consideration. A part of the facilitation skill is to find the mechanisms that will be most effective, depending upon the size of the team and the nature of the issue.

IN PRACTICE

As part of the introduction to a workshop it is useful to introduce the concept of the workshop 'as a place to think' and then set some ground rules along the lines of:

- everyone speaks and everyone is heard
- a speaker should be allowed to finish their thought; talking over someone else or interrupting destroys the thought
- all thoughts are considered to have equal value, irrespective of grade or status
- celebrate the fact that there are other perspectives in the room, rather than resisting or opposing them, and
- lower your sense of urgency, park the to-do list and let your mind expand.

This is your contract with the room. When dialogue turns to debate, people go off agenda, or start talking over each other you can take them back to the contract and reset the room once again to a thinking environment.

Some additional thoughts on facilitating a thinking environment.

1. Try and stay out of the way. If you want to encourage the team to think you must pose the right questions and then leave them to it. As facilitator it is not your role to lead or dominate the discussion. If you are the team leader this can be very hard and so it takes self-discipline to hold back your own thoughts and opinions at least until everyone else has spoken.

2. Hold the structure. The facilitation role requires you to develop the structure for the thinking session usually expressed as an agenda. You are the person who then maintains the structure of the session as it rolls out ensuring the right behavioural norms are maintained, interruptions and talking over others is minimized, and key ideas are noted.

3. A thinking session might take place as an item in a team meeting or as a full day workshop. The point is that someone takes the role of thinking facilitator for the session. This does not necessarily have to be you. In teams experienced in working as a collaborative unit, another team member might take on this role allowing you to participate.

4. Don't overprotect. If the team appears to be struggling to make any progress in their thinking it can be tempting to step in. Contain your instinct to intervene, as the best thinking will happen when the team have to work at the issue. New ways of seeing a situation can take time to emerge so be patient and keep nudging them to keep exploring ideas and options. It may sometimes be necessary to jolt them out of following the easy options by challenging them to contemplate more extreme alternatives.

SLOW DOWN TO SPEED UP

WHAT IS THE TECHNIQUE?

This technique is a process of resisting the urge to launch straight into task completion and instead put some time, both as an individual and as a team, into planning how the team are going to work together and helping establish the conditions for success. The basic concept is that by investing in thinking and planning at the start, the team can deliver its objectives more quickly, through better communication, trusting relationships and fewer mistakes.

WHY IS IT USEFUL?

An important element of the team coaching/leadership role is to guide the team to collectively take time at the start of the project to work through the potential challenges ahead and take steps to mitigate them. Slowing down at the start has the following benefits.

- It helps focus the team on the challenges ahead and how to deal with them effectively.
- It creates space to establish the desired behavioural norms.
- It encourages you to clear your own mind to see the way forward.
- It gives the team greater clarity and purpose.

Practising the technique of actively slowing the pace helps resist the common tendency to leap into action as soon as a project or initiative is given the green light to proceed. Not only will this technique save the wasted time and effort needed to redo work that needs correcting, but it will also prompt the team to anticipate future challenges.

Slow thinking also allows you to collectively work through some of the softer issues around personality and individual motivation. A team that understands each other's mental filters and perceptions has a greater chance of forming a cohesive and resilient group than one where such personal attributes are taken for granted.

THE THEORY

There is a slightly annoying saying that 'if you fail to plan you are planning to fail'. It is also annoyingly true. Past experience repeatedly tells us that when something has gone wrong with a new project or initiative, a bit more thought applied at the start would have saved a lot of stress later on. So if we know we need to spend more time in planning and preparation, why don't we do it?

There are a number of reasons for this phenomenon. John McGuire and Vance Tang (2011) make the observation that the complexity and uncertainty of modern life creates situations in which managers often feel that they have lost control. In their attempt to find some clarity, they try to move faster only to find that they have merely created more uncertainty. McGuire and Tang put forward the idea that complex problems require 90% enquiry and 10% decision-making. It is important to first collect the necessary data to see what is going on, and then take the time to think through what the information generated actually means.

Another reason why we often fail to plan is that thinking is often hard work. Daniel Kahneman (2011) writes about the tendency of people to rely on instinctive judgement (thinking fast) over rational analysis (thinking slow). His explanation is that thinking actually requires a lot of energy and so when we are tired or under pressure, we revert to the easier cognitive mechanisms. The problem with relying on our intuition, when dealing with a new problem, is that whilst we may make quick decisions, if we don't have all of the right information, we often make poor choices.

Humans are also well known for a tendency towards optimism bias, where we intuitively believe that everything will somehow or other turn out fine. Whilst optimism in itself is an admirable quality, optimism bias shuts out our ability to question the assumptions that we are making. We press on in wilful ignorance of issues and obstacles that quickly slow our progress. Slow thinking requires checking our biases and assumptions, and acknowledging that there may be additional information that needs to be considered. In the project arena, slow thinking has the greatest impact at the start, when plans are being worked up.

IN PRACTICE

There is a phrase that comes from the PRINCE2 methodology, which refers to a project stage called Phase Zero. This is the section of the project when the team is assembled and the project planning begins. It is Phase Zero rather than Phase One because the implication is that it is not a full-on, action and delivery stage of the project. The output from Phase Zero is more about how the team will work together rather than what they will be doing.

In the Assess section of the toolkit you will find a number of activities you can work on, firstly by yourself and then subsequently with the team. Tools such as the 'cup of tea meeting' (**Tool 4**) are a good illustration of my point. Taking time to meet some of the core team and have an informal chat about the project gives you the quiet, unpressured space to give people time to think.

The slow phase is also the opportunity for you to start to shape the behavioural norms of the team and put in place the different procedures and other elements that are going to become part of your team's internal process. Much of this work needs to be done in a workshop towards the end of Phase Zero where you can work through a number of the elements I have described in the 'Set-up' section of the toolkit.

RESIST THE PRESSURE

You may sometimes feel under pressure from the project sponsors to demonstrate some form of immediate action. This pressure should be avoided by explaining to the sponsor in advance how the project is going to be planned. I came across a project manager from Germany who told me she hated wasting time. Her philosophy was that if you rush into a project without thinking you end up making mistakes, and must then go back and start the tasks again. She would therefore try to resist any pressure from her clients to respond to their sense of urgency. She would often take up to a fortnight, working with the team, planning as much of the detail as possible, thinking about the challenges ahead, and how to work around them. By getting everyone working together as a thinking team at the start, she believes that trust and communication develop more quickly and so, once the team get moving, they have shorter, more productive meetings and can make much quicker decisions. She claims that when she gets this planning time with the team, more often than not her projects finish ahead of schedule.

CURIOUS ENQUIRY

WHAT IS CURIOUS ENQUIRY?

The shift in mindset that allows you to gain information from other members of the team by having a genuine curiosity to learn what they have to say.

WHY IS IT USEFUL?

By asking questions in a manner that is genuinely curious, you will encourage the team to say what they really think. This process encourages upward communication, providing you with a much fuller picture of what is happening within the team and provides a wider range of potential solutions to the challenges that need to be met.

THE THEORY

Many societies have a problem establishing effective two-way communication. Communication patterns are typically built around a hierarchical model where those in authority tell their subordinates what to do. The command and control culture so prevalent in many Western organizations is built on the assumption that the leader or manager has more knowledge of a particular issue than the person who must take action. In a complex situation, however, this assumption is no longer correct as, by definition, there are too many variables for any one person to have all of the information needed to make a decision.

The concept of curious enquiry starts with the recognition that you must acknowledge a potential weakness in your position. In other words, your subordinate may have more information than you. By accepting that you may have less information than the team working for you, you do in fact put yourself in a potentially stronger position. By drawing out more information you are likely to make better decisions, leading to more successful outcomes.

This can be difficult for many managers where the culture of the organization is built upon the concept of the heroic leader or firms where technical knowledge and skill are seen as a fundamental requirement for career advancement.

IN PRACTICE

Being curious can be difficult if you are used to seeing yourself, or alternatively are seen by your team, as being the smartest person in the room. The technique of curious enquiry requires you to begin important conversations with the initial stance that you are partially ignorant and that others in the team have a perspective or information that you currently do not possess. As Ed Schein (2013) explains, you must become temporarily dependent and vulnerable.

This temporary subordination helps create an environment of psychological safety for the other person increasing the chances they will tell you what you need to know. It sends a signal that you are willing to listen and empowers the other individual. By asking questions using an approach that shows real interest and

The switch from command and control to curious enquiry is not always smooth. It may take some time for the team to adjust to your new approach. I have a coaching client, David, who was concerned that none of his line managers seemed able to make decisions for themselves. Every morning there was a queue at his door to resolve daily problems leaving little time to do the other tasks required to grow his business. After some discussion on curious enquiry, he decided to try and change his approach. The following day his production manager came to see him with a number of issues to resolve. Instead of his usual habit of making a series of ad hoc decisions, David asked, 'I don't know, what do you think?' The manager was completely taken by surprise and stumbled uncomfortably through some half thoughts before making a hasty exit. Later that day one of David's co-directors came to ask if he was feeling unwell as word had got around the production facility that he was 'behaving a bit odd!'

I provide this story as an illustration that there are few magic bullets. The lack of immediate success tempted David to revert to his old 'do and tell' style. He realized, however, that his ambitions for his business would not be achieved if his line managers were not able to take more ownership of the decision-making for their parts of the business. I am pleased to say that he has stuck with the technique and slowly, but steadily, the business has been transformed and David reports a much better balance in how issues are discussed and decisions made.

curiosity, you set the grounds for developing much stronger inter-personal relationships.

For example, a curious enquiry might start with the admission, 'I am a bit stuck here. I really don't know the answer so I would like to hear what you think.' Be careful with your tone and inflections. Your curious questions can easily be interpreted as sarcasm or be seen to be leading to some other yet to be revealed agenda.

Technique 5

INFLUENTIAL QUESTIONS

WHAT IS AN INFLUENTIAL QUESTION?

The technique of influencing the behavioural norms of a team by asking questions.

WHY IS IT USEFUL?

It is thought to be nearly impossible for one person to force another to change how they think. You might achieve a short-term shift in observable behaviour through the use of force, either through threat or persuasion. Without a shift in thinking, however, we soon revert to our original behaviour once the force is removed.

Influential questions are therefore a useful mechanism for steering the conversation to encourage the other person or team to arrive at your conclusion for themselves.

THE THEORY

When we want someone to change behaviours, all too often we try to persuade others to see what we understand to be the cold, hard logic of the situation. The problem is that what seems to be logical to us may be merely viewed as circumstantial evidence by the other party. We each see the world through our own mental filters. These filters form continually throughout our lives shaping our beliefs and opinions. They dictate what information we decide is important and what can be disregarded. They govern what we believe, what we value and how we make sense of the world around us. It is therefore often the case that two people can examine the same situation and yet come to an entirely different conclusion as to its meaning.

Some of the filters are deep and fixed and are therefore almost impossible to change. Others are less embedded, being more about habit than fixed belief. It is therefore feasible for people to change or adjust the filters that govern perspectives and issues that they have not really considered. As a coach you have the opportunity to shift some of these filters so that they align more closely to your own perspective.

The more you understand about another person's drivers, the easier it is to find a question that will get through their initial filters and nudge them to the look at a situation from a different perspective.

IN PRACTICE

There is an important distinction to be made between the curious enquiry mindset explained in **Technique 4** and influential questions. Both forms of questioning require an open and enquiring approach but influential questions nudge the respondent down a particular line of enquiry. *Influential* questions should nevertheless be distinguished from *leading* questions. A leading question along the lines of 'didn't you realize that there would be a problem if you did that?' is very direct and can really only elicit one response. Leading questions do not help people adjust their filters.

The key to the technique lies in how you phrase the question. Influential questioning must encourage the other party to genuinely think about the options and how they might articulate the solution. This is the critical component and so when, where, and how you ask influential questions is important. If you want someone to think, then try and ensure they have the time and space to allow their minds to process new lines of thought. Influential questioning is not a hurried process. You must try and help the other party work through an issue to find the root cause of any peculiar beliefs or biases they might have developed, and then find a way of articulating them.

Thinking requires effort and so your choice of time and location are important. Noisy pubs or cafes are not usually the best place for either party to think or listen attentively. Avoid an urgent environment where the focus is on action. Far better to find the space for reflection. This is why workshops are much better than team meetings for helping teams reflect and use their imagination. As a team coach you also need to ensure that the environment feels safe. It is very difficult to influence someone to contemplate changes in their mindset when they are fearful of ridicule or other perceived threat.

Examples of influential questions are:

- What would happen if…?
- How do you feel we should approach this problem?
- Where did you have to deal with this problem before and what happened?
- What did you learn from…?

The tone and emphasis of your questions is important. You will be more influential when you ask questions in a calm, neutral manner. The other party needs to feel that you are genuinely interested in what they think.

Influential questions also work well in steering a discussion. Instead of dictating to the team that they must take a particular course of action, you can make a statement along the lines of 'so I am wondering what the potential benefits of adopting action x might be'. In asking the question using a tone of genuine enquiry, you are likely to stimulate the team to switch their thinking to the positive benefits that might occur if you choose a particular path of action.

> My old mentor, Jimmy James, once asked me what was more important to me: to take the credit for my ideas, or to see them being implemented. His point was one should try to plant the seed of an idea in someone else's mind, and then allow them to grow it. Not only would they feel greater ownership of the idea, but it would obviously have your support and so would then have a much better chance of success.

Notice that you have not asked for a decision. You have simply asked them to bring out the reasons why it might be a good idea. Having brought the group to a place where they now feel they have a share in creating the idea, you have a much better chance of their agreement.

They are also far more likely to own the implementation.

LISTENING FOR CLUES

WHAT IS THE TECHNIQUE?

The habit of gathering all available data when listening to an individual or a group.

WHY IS IT USEFUL?

The more information we can gather, the more likely we will be able to make better decisions. We are typically poor, however, at taking in all of the information being presented to us when another person is speaking. The reality for many of us is that listening is often simply a pause for breath whilst we think of what we are going to say next. This technique is a reminder to work harder at picking up just what is being communicated.

THE THEORY

To help a team you need to understand what is going on within the team's inter-personal dynamics. If you don't pick up the clues, then you risk ignoring the signals telling you what is working and what might be getting in the way. Alternatively you may be making too many incorrect assumptions.

Listening is a skill taken for granted. It is easy to assume it is just about hearing. Simply taking in the words of others is effectively just data. To turn the data into information, it needs to be processed to find the patterns that will make sense. Business practice, particularly in Western societies, has increasingly become a 'tell' rather than a 'listen' culture, which puts more value on what we say over the thoughts and interpretations of others. We need to relearn how to listen. As children, we often listen attentively as we try to understand and learn from what goes on around us, but as adults we seem to lose that part of the communication equation.

We don't just listen with our ears. The eyes have an important role as well. When someone is focused and talking intently their bodies reveal additional information, some of which may actually contradict the words you are hearing. Body language can be expressed in many different ways. How people subconsciously use hands, arms, shoulders and facial muscles will help reveal many of the emotions attached to the words.

Similarly the pitch and tone of the speaker voice may add additional information. There is a lot of additional data available to you, provided you make the effort to look for it.

IN PRACTICE

The starting point is to recognize that listening is an active rather than a passive activity. When someone is expressing themselves on an important issue, you need to focus on what is actually being said rather than what you have instinctively assumed is being meant. This is particularly important when you ask a question. As discussed in **Technique 5**, good questions are often the key to helping shift someone's thinking. The question is, however, only half of the process. To encourage someone to think out loud, they need to know you are listening.

The best way to show someone that you have their undivided attention is to keep your face focused on the talker. Often, when we are thinking out loud, our eyes and face may move to one side as we search for the right words to explain our thoughts. Our peripheral vision, however, tells us whether the listener is still focused on us, or is looking away, glancing at their watch or phone or being distracted by other movements in the room.

I have found that staring directly into the speakers eye's can be a bit disconcerting for them and so my preference is to look at a space about 6 inches in front of their nose. I keep my movement as still as possible and try to let the speaker know they have my full and undivided attention. The same principle applies to working with a group, in that you simply switch the direction in which you are facing to listen to whoever is speaking.

Nancy Kline, in the fabulous book *Time to Think* (1999) recommends that the coach practises their 'listening face'. This is the expression you hope will tell the speaker you are intent upon understanding their point without making any judgement. She makes the point, however, that you should practise in front of a mirror. What may feel like rapt attention to you may come across as something very different to the speaker.

Active listening applies both in a one-on-one situation but also to the team. When someone is speaking, if they know you are listening they are more likely to get to the point. You also, however, need to pick up the signals coming from the others around the table. Who is engaged, who is supportive and who is agitated by what is being said? The team will continually give off signals, which may not always be strong, but are nevertheless present.

Perhaps the most important point is to try and avoid the temptation to interrupt. Irrespective of your good intentions, when someone pauses, it does not mean they have stopped thinking. They will signal when they are ready to re-engage. Remember a good question often opens up new channels of thought, and so the speaker may need some space to continue to think. Don't be discomforted by silence.

ONLY CLUES

It is useful to regularly remind yourself that most of the signals you are picking up are only clues to help you decipher what people *really* think. As time goes on you will start to recognize the patterns of behaviour that provide indicators of what might be going through someone's mind. The important thing is not to jump to conclusions. If certain behaviour is getting in the way of the team's performance, ask what is going on. So pose a question along the lines of 'so I notice when X happens, you often do Y. Why is that?' Then listen and see what further clues are revealed.

ADOPT AN 'AGILE' MINDSET

WHAT IS AN 'AGILE' MINDSET?

An 'Agile' mindset is a way of thinking that encourages both the coach/leader and the team to adopt a different perspective on how they work together.

WHY IS IT USEFUL?

'Agile' thinking encourages flexibility in how you see the challenges of working in an unpredictable environment. The principles of 'Agile' thinking sit very comfortably with the underlying philosophy of team coaching, particularly in the need to pay attention to team behavioural process as well as task delivery.

THE THEORY

Mindset is a way of thinking and perceiving which all humans use to make sense of the world. Developing an 'Agile' mindset requires a shift in the convention of 'cause and effect' thinking to be able to adapt more quickly to the paradoxical challenges created by complexity.

'Agile' (Beck *et al.*, 2001) has become a popular term used in many different contexts to encourage speed and flexibility. Originating in the software industry it is used to describe everything from management techniques to organizational culture. In the context of team coaching, however, an 'Agile' mindset has relatively little to do with process and is more concerned with perspective.

It is worth going back to the original source of the 'Agile' movement and the manifesto that established a new way of working on complex projects. If you are not familiar with the story, the Agile Manifesto was created by a group of software engineers who met in a ski resort in Utah in 2001.

They were seeking a solution to the slow and cumbersome methodologies that were the norm at that time. To respect their thinking I have replicated the manifesto in the diagram below.

The Agile Manifesto

We are uncovering better ways of developing software by doing it and helping others do it. Through this work we have come to value:

Individuals and interactions
over processes and tools

Working software
over comprehensive documentation

Customer collaboration
over contract negotiation

Responding to change
over following a plan

That is, while there is value in the items on the right, we value the items on the left more.

© Beck *et al.*, 2001
This declaration may be freely copied in any form, but only in its entirety through this notice.

The authors of the manifesto formed a non-profit organization with the objective of promoting their revolutionary concept to the wider software community. The concept has subsequently led to fundamental change in how teams of software engineers work. Ralph Stacey (2003) makes the observation that all major projects now tend to exist in a space somewhere between order and chaos. He makes the case that in such an environment the traditional mechanisms for progressing a major initiative have a much lower chance of working. Over the past five years, the 'Agile' concept has therefore spread beyond the information technology sector and is now a common point of discussion in project management and leadership thinking.

IN PRACTICE

If you don't work in the software industry you might well ask what has the Agile Manifesto got to do with team coaching? The 'Agile' mindset helps set your approach and attitude. In the dual role of coach and leader your style adjusts to adopt the principles set out in the box to the circumstances of your mission. The 'Agile' approach provides a team coach with four principles which alter the way in which everyone involved in the project looks at the challenge and understands where the priorities should lie. Below I explain each of these principles in turn.

'Individual and interactions over process and tools' establishes the principle that attention needs to be paid to the social connections between people, rather than focusing predominantly on procedure.

'Working software over comprehensive documentation' reminds the team that it is the outcome that is important not the route chosen to get there. This pragmatic perspective is fundamental to the coaching ethos in helping a team work through complex challenges.

'Customer collaboration over contract negotiation' attempts to rebalance the tendency to resort to the transactional behaviour associated with initiatives and projects that are merely complicated (see **Technique 10** – 'Developing your maturity in complexity').

'Responding to change over following a plan' establishes a new principle that accepts the future is unpredictable and so teams must be able to work though a number of iterations testing their output against stakeholder needs as the work progresses.

It should be emphasized that process, plans and documents are not ignored in the 'Agile' approach. They just do not dominate the team's focus and priorities.

Lyssa Adkins (2010) believes that 'Agile' leadership requires both coaching and mentoring support. She makes the distinction that coaching includes those activities that involve helping the team to work as an effective unit. Mentoring is then required on an individual-by-individual basis to keep them aligned to the team's agreed methods and collaborative practices. If you are interested in exploring 'Agile' as it applies outside the software industry there is plenty of information available both in print and online. *Coaching Agile Teams* by Lyssa Adkins (referenced Chapter 9) is a good place to start.

Whatever your source of information, don't get distracted by the references to software engineering jargon such as scrum user stories and sprints. Stay focused on the principles of the Agile Manifesto and work out how they apply to your industry/sector/task.

USING CASE STORIES

WHAT IS THE TECHNIQUE?

The use of stories to help teams envisage the future, make sense of the present and learn from the past. Most people are familiar with the idea of a case study. This is usually an exercise in assembling facts, explaining events and then stating the outcome. Case studies are almost always devoid of personality. *Case stories* are therefore different. They resonate with us primarily because the human element is at the heart of the tale.

WHY IS IT USEFUL?

We know that storytelling has been an important mechanism for passing on important messages for thousands of years. Humans in every part of the globe can point to a time, before the printed word, where stories were used to pass knowledge down from generation to generation. Stories can take many forms, from simple recollections of past events, to hypothetical scenarios which stretch our imagination. Stories can engage, excite and inspire us. They can also be used to warn of the consequences of certain behaviours. Stories can also scare us into taking action and can even help modify behaviour.

In times of continuous uncertainty and disruptive change, it is important to be able to connect with the people in and around your team, so the group have a common view of the journey ahead. In an age where we are frequently overwhelmed by information, it can be difficult to find the mental bandwidth to be able to create or receive clear and memorable messages. Information is compressed into lists of bullet points and graphs, but leaves little sense of meaning.

Stories have been found to be one of the most effective mechanisms for explaining complicated themes in a way that not only makes sense but, crucially, is also memorable. Stories talk to both the conscious and the unconscious mind, stirring emotions and drawing us in. They are a useful mechanism for slowing the pace of the team's early activity and encouraging them to think and plan.

THE THEORY

Recent advances in neuroscience have started to shed some light on why stories work as well as they do. When we listen to a story the parts of our brains that deal with language processing become activated to decode the meaning. This happens when we start to take in any form of new information, but when we hear a story our emotions also become aroused, stimulating a wider potential range of response. Feel good chemicals such as serotonin, dopamine and oxytocin are produced as we react to thoughts that resonate with our own experiences.

Stories often tend to have a stronger resonance when we hear them directly from the mouth of the speaker. Other media such as print, radio or television can each be powerful mediums for transmitting emotions, but the effect of listening to someone in the same room creates a two-way reaction which forms a strong bond. Scientists have identified a neurological phenomenon called 'mirror neurons' where the neurons active in the storyteller's brain also fire off the same neurons in the listener's brain. As we recount an adventure, our memories are stimulated and so as we describe what happened, the audience subconsciously starts to feel some of our experience.

IN PRACTICE

Using stories to shape team behaviours requires a number of elements. Firstly, your story needs to be relevant. In your role as team coach, your focus is on the team as an entity and its goals and objectives. The stories chosen or requested should support that prime objective. They can be used in a project set-up meeting, or even during team meetings, but they are most effective when everyone is focused on a particular theme or exercise.

The more authentic we believe the story to be, the more resonance it is likely to have. Remember, it makes no difference if the stories are embellished or not. They are not case studies. The purpose of the story is to establish the underlying messages of good versus bad, right versus wrong, and success versus failure. These case stories lead us to a place where difficult issues become clearer as we learn how others dealt with similar situations. Stories also have a role in unravelling complexity. Humans are very good at filling in the information around a story without needing to have everything described in detail. We are able to recognize the complexity of relationships around the situation being described to us without having to stop and try and understand how those variables affect the outcome. The story also needs to catch the listener's imagination. The introduction of the characters of the hero, villain or guardian will help the story resonate. It is worth providing some background information that will give these characters some personality, allowing your audience to find some context.

LISTEN TO WHAT ELSE IS BEING REVEALED

Whenever I interview someone as part of my research into team dynamics, I ask them first to tell me about a team experience that was either memorably good or memorably bad. I have found this to be a particularly effective way of getting my interviewee engaged in the topic. It also nearly always produces an amazing story. It should not be surprising, but invariably the story will focus around a project or situation which was almost, but not quite, impossible, and how the team rose to the challenge. Alternatively it may be a story of complacency and opportunity squandered. These stories not only provide me with some additional research material, but also give me a degree of insight into the storyteller. When a story arouses emotion in the teller, you are given some clues as to what is important to him or to her. A choice of emphasis on some aspect of the story may indicate particular preferences, or perspectives that may be worth following up later. Stories are also a good way of revealing your own vulnerabilities, which may encourage others to open up.

Finally, take care not to fall into the trap of reminiscing about 'the good old days'. Anecdotal tales of simpler times in the past will do little to help a team looking for answers to complexity. So pick your stories with some care. The bottom line should always be 'so what can we learn from that experience that will be of use to us today?' (See **Tool 27**.)

THE IMPORTANCE OF VISUAL INFORMATION

WHAT IS THE TECHNIQUE?

Using white space – either on paper, flip charts or whiteboards – to create ad hoc images that help the team to articulate thoughts and ideas in a structured way.

WHY IS IT USEFUL?

Too many meetings rely on reports and slideshow presentations as the primary means of communication. This approach assumes everyone has read the documents and understands every bullet point, in enough detail to fully understand the issues under discussion. The process may be effective in disseminating information, but rarely provides the stimulation needed to find answers to difficult problems.

To engage the team, it is often more effective to build a discussion around images, words and signs created in the moment, that everyone can see. Using flip charts, whiteboards, or even large pieces of paper helps everyone focus on the specific questions or points being made.

In workshops, and other types of 'thinking' sessions, clear wall space is an essential element for recording thoughts and ideas from everyone in the room, not just the people who like talking.

There are many different benefits to using visuals to articulate and capture information and ideas. These include the following.

- *Points of focus* - using single words or images or symbols helps the speaker focus on finding the heart of the issue and keeps the discussion focused on the issue. This helps avoid the tendency to move off topic into peripheral areas.
- *Engagement* – noting key points encourages participation and a non-judgemental way of acknowledging what has been said and how it was heard.
- *Spontane*ity – contributions can be made as thoughts occur and do not require people to wait for a formal turn.
- *Finding connections* – ideas are allowed to build and connections to be made. The conversation can be non-linear allowing creative thoughts to be noted for further development.

THE THEORY

Visual images help us in our search for the patterns of activity that help us make sense of complicated situations. When text and images are combined they allow the integration of thinking from both the left and right hemisphere, creating stronger more memorable output. David Sibbet (2010), an expert visual communicator, believes that all humans have the ability to draw. It is just that the majority of us stop trying to draw around the age of seven or eight years old. It appears that when we realize we cannot create an accurate interpretation of the image in our minds, we give up trying. It is worth noting, however, that simple images are often better at conveying a message than more accurate or complicated drawings. Cartoons, for example, engage us because we have to work a bit harder to recognize what the images are doing.

Humans are wired to try and make sense of whatever we see, so that symbols, even vague squiggles on a page, will be interpreted as meaning something. For example, simple stick figures will add a human element, as will happy or sad faces. Arrows give direction of travel and boxes and circles provide the envelopes for distinct themes and ideas. We are not therefore unduly worried by graphic accuracy. The mind is capable of filling in the gaps for itself. Graphic metaphors allow people to explain how they make sense of the situation.

Sibbet also picks up on a more subtle point that people are more likely to adopt ideas they feel have come from within the group rather than from outside, even from experts. He makes the observation that when a group sees its work recorded, their trust in its validity increases and the group will use the charts and graphics they have created as their collective memory.

IN PRACTICE

There is an obvious but often overlooked practical challenge to using visual information, which is to ensure that there is something to write on and also something to write with. So plan ahead. When you have the choice, ensure there are flip charts and/or wall space available. I have learned the hard way not to trust the marker pens left in the room, and now carry my own set of flip chart pens as well as a set of whiteboard markers. I also carry a pack of 'white tack' to allow flip charts to be posted on a wall or other surface (subject of course to the property manager not getting sniffy about possibly defacing the walls).

I try and work to a rough ratio of one flip chart for every six people in the room. This provides a facility to quickly break into sub-groups and create images around which you can progress discussion. This brings us to the question of meeting space. Again, given the choice, choose a room which is big enough for the team to stand up and move around.

Whiteboards are a great invention, the bigger the better. When looking at complex problems with multiple elements, it is helpful to put some thought into the structure before you start. This gives you the visual framework within, allowing the team to work though ideas which are often disconnected, without the need to follow any particular logical progression.

CREATE A CANVAS

I sometimes find it useful to print out large A1 or A0 size sheets of paper that are pre-designed so that the structure or headings are set, but there is still plenty of space for the team's thoughts. These sheets are useful when you want to generate a lot of thinking around specific issues (see **Tool 17** – 'The collaboration canvas'). An extension of the canvas concept is to use a large roll of paper, such as that used in a drawing plotter, that is long enough to fill the width of a room, upon which to build a large graphic containing all the information generated. I have seen some great examples of strategic vision being dissected into a range of tactical plans and activities all summarized on a single sheet. For some events where there is a strong need for team cohesion, it is even worth employing a visual specialist who will help build the images as the discussion is developed.

OUTPUT

At the end of the session we will have a huge amount of information up on the wall allowing us to see the whole issue and then decide how we can then dissect and communicate it. It is, however, only of value if you actually do something with the information generated. Visual images are easy to capture, particularly now that most people have a camera readily to hand in their phone or tablet. Action lists can be quickly written up or circulated without the need to carry large volumes of paper home at the end of the meeting.

As mentioned above, the notes and drawings generated at team meetings and workshops become the collective memory of the team, but only if they feel they are a progression towards the team's goal. For example, when we run a project workshop, particularly a kick-off event where the team come together for the first time, we turn the images into a project handbook (**Tool 20**). So as soon as the event finishes the notes are compiled into a text document or slide deck, and are circulated the next day.

DEVELOPING YOUR MATURITY IN COMPLEXITY

WHAT IS THE TECHNIQUE?

The ability to look at any situation and recognize the range of variables that are likely to affect the potential outcome, and to then help the team come to a decision without resorting to over-simplification.

WHY IS IT USEFUL?

In the 21st century, the environment in which organizations and teams must work is much less stable than conditions in the previous century. Leaders and managers need to be able to become comfortable in recognizing that decisions must be made where the result is uncertain, but at least take the team in the right direction.

THE THEORY

Complexity is the buzzword of the last decade. Overused and in danger of becoming treated as jargon, it is nevertheless an important concept. There is a considerable volume of academic literature on the topic of complexity, and the theoretical science that attempts to make sense of the challenges it creates. It is, however, a very practical component of our working lives. Complexity is also contextual and so it can be difficult to pin down in general discussion. The starting point is to make the distinction between issues that are complex and those that are merely complicated.

Complicated problems are difficult to work out initially, but once we see the patterns of activity, we can find the answer. Humans are good at spotting patterns. We look for them all of the time, and tend to use pattern recognition as a primary problem-solving mechanism. The challenge with complexity arises when there are too many variables in play for our minds to extrapolate how a situation will evolve. The transactional response is to try to simplify complex issues by ignoring those aspects of a problem that we do not understand.

A common illustration is to compare flying a large commercial airliner with the task of controlling air traffic. Enter the cockpit of a modern aeroplane and you are presented with an array of switches, levers and dials presenting a novice with a bewildering range of options. To an experienced pilot who knows the function of each mechanism, there is a predictable pattern of activity. She knows that provided the switches and levers are operated in the correct sequence, the plane will take off and land largely as anticipated. Controlling a commercial airliner is therefore merely complicated. Contrast this with the complexity of trying to manage the traffic in the skies around a large airport hub. Controlling the safe arrival and departure of commercial aircraft requires a strong awareness of the likely weather conditions that an aeroplane will encounter on its journey around the world. There are so many factors that can affect our atmosphere that even the most powerful computers cannot accurately predict exactly how the weather in a particular region will behave. All the forecasters can do is make their best estimate and adapt in real time as the journeys play out.

IN PRACTICE

Complex situations require a different approach to the management of people and projects. There is a strong consensus that collaborative teamwork will produce a better answer to a complex problem. Since, by definition, you cannot accurately predict what is going to happen in a complex situation, the traditional approach to planning activities or programmes becomes obsolete. The process instead requires moving forward in a series of iterations or steps, pausing at the end of each step to agree the next stage, based on whatever new information is to hand. This approach requires a different style of leadership where there is less reliance on the heroic individual and more value is placed on drawing out observations, thoughts and ideas from the team.

The longer term challenge is to develop your own maturity in complexity. Maturity can be defined as 'a quality or state of being mature, of behaving mentally and emotionally as an adult'. Maturity is generally seen as a positive quality. It is associated with wisdom and is one of the relatively few attributes that can improve with age. However, not every 60-year-old is mature. You need to work at it. The attributes that I would associate with maturity in complexity include:

- the patience to pull back and see the bigger picture
- an ability to manage your emotions in difficult situations, thus maintaining the capacity to think rationally.
- the habit of thinking systemically and seeking to understand an issue from a range of perspectives
- the humility to see your own contribution as part of a whole, and
- the habit of continually seeking to learn from recent experience and help others adapt to the future.

This is not a complete list, as it is intended to paint a picture of maturity rather than a specification.

One of the most important shifts for a leader/manager is to learn to become comfortable with the reality that you cannot, and should not, expect to know all of the answers. It is a recognition that your relationship with the team is interdependent, i.e. you are as dependent upon them for the success of your venture

> An illustration of maturity In complexity is a story I came across in my research, of an experienced manager who had a reputation for delivering successful cross-functional initiatives. The feedback from one of his team was that he never seemed to get angry or frustrated when events did not go as planned. He simply acknowledged the problem and then focused everyone's attention on what they might do to work around it. He invested time early in the project getting to know the key stakeholders and trying to understand what really mattered to them. He paid attention to building support for the project and was always somehow able to influence other managers to provide extra resources just when they were needed. As a coach he had a calming effect on the team and gave them confidence that, whatever the problem, together they would find a solution.

as they are upon you. In a complex environment, you need to develop a different relationship to that of a command and control leader. To make decisions you need to make use of the judgement of the wider team, rather than following your own 'gut feel'. In such situations you are unlikely to have all of the information/experience that typically forms the basis for intuitive decision-making. This links to the technique of learning how to ask genuinely curious questions and then improving your skills in listening to the answers you are given.

SECTION THREE

Team Coaching Tools

The tools set out on the following pages are designed around the model of team coaching explained in chapter 3. They broadly follow the sequence set out in the diagram below, in that the Assess and Set-up tools are usually used at the beginning of the team's life cycle whilst the other tools are probably more useful once the team has become established. However, do not feel tied to this structure as you are likely to find that some tools will work at earlier or later stages than the position that I have allocated them in the model.

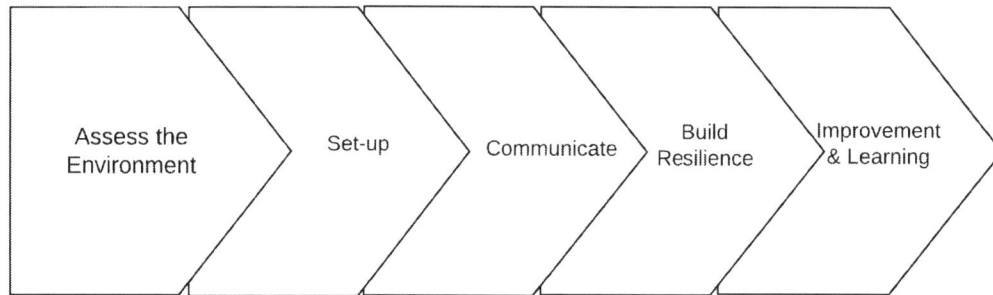

Assess the Environment ⟩ Set-up ⟩ Communicate ⟩ Build Resilience ⟩ Improvement & Learning

Figure 2 – Team coaching model

The tools are arranged as follows:

Tools 1 to 9	Tools for assessing the team's environment
Tools 10 to 20	Tools for setting up an effective team
Tools 21 to 31	Tools for improving communication
Tools 32 to 38	Tools for building team resilience
Tools 39 to 45	Tools for improvement and team learning

The tools provide a structure around which to stimulate discussion that will engage the team leading to commitment, focus and increasing levels of trust. The tools are therefore designed to provide you with a range of mechanisms to help you work more effectively with your team. They are nevertheless skeletal structures which lack the context of your specific circumstances. It is for you to decide how to adapt each tool to suit your team's needs.

Chapter 4

TOOLS FOR ASSESSING THE TEAM'S ENVIRONMENT

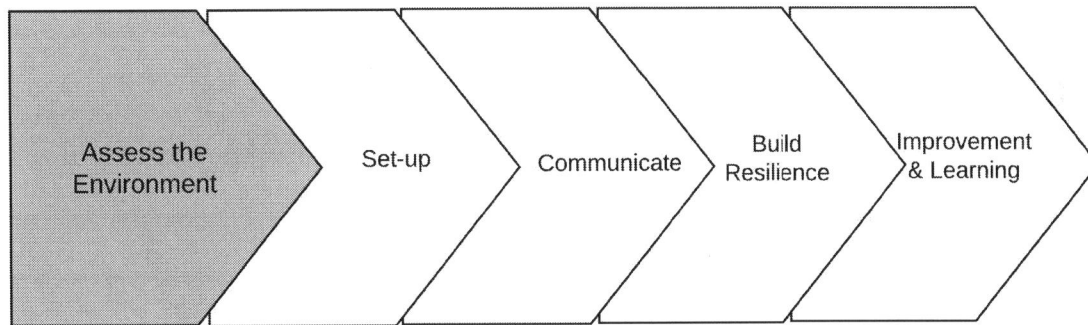

```
Assess the          Set-up      Communicate     Build      Improvement
Environment                                   Resilience    & Learning
```

Figure 2A – Team coaching model: Assess the environment

Tool 1	Complex or simply complicated
Tool 2	Assess the project environment
Tool 3	Articulating stakeholder paradoxes
Tool 4	The 'cup of tea meeting'
Tool 5	Acknowledging cultural diversity
Tool 6	Dangerous assumptions and leaps of faith
Tool 7	Roles not jobs
Tool 8	Force field analysis
Tool 9	Surviving the storming stage

TOOL 1 – IS YOUR PROJECT COMPLEX OR SIMPLY COMPLICATED?

PURPOSE

- To make the team and/or the project sponsor aware of the degree of complexity of the project.
- To increase awareness of the need to work collaboratively.

Time required: 15–30 minutes.

THE THEORY

A common reason for project failure is the mistaken assumption that traditional transactional mechanisms and behaviours, which may work on a complicated project, will also achieve the desired outcome on a complex project.

The research on effective teams highlights the need for teams to adopt collaborative working methods when a project becomes complex. There are many ways of trying to define the distinction between complicated and complex but, to avoid getting lost in the semantics of language, table 4 below allows the team to quickly work out whether the problem/project requires a collaborative approach.

THE TOOL

Step 1. Print off a copy of the table for each member of the team, or download it from the website www.teamcoachingtoolkit.com/toolkit/project-complex-simply-complicated/

Step 2. Ask each person to independently rate the project/problem. This should take no more than five minutes.

76

Step 3. Draw up a three column by six row blank table on a flip chart and work down the table asking each member to say where they think the project sits against each of the criteria.

Step 4. Assess the results and start a discussion as to what the practical difference between complicated and complex means for your project.

Simple	Complicated	Complex
We have done this before and we know exactly what to do	We have done something similar before so we have some idea as to what to do	We have never done this before and need to work out a completely new solution
We only need to consult with one key stakeholder	We need to consult with two key stakeholders	We need to consult with three or more key stakeholders
There is no real time pressure to complete the task	There is a moderate degree of urgency to complete the task	Completing the task is business critical and has a high degree of urgency
The people needed to work on this task are all based in one location	The people needed to work on this task are based in two different locations	The people needed to work on this task are based in three or more different locations
The task requires limited specialist technical input	The task requires specialist input from up to three technical specialists	The task requires specialist input from up to four or more technical specialists

Table 4 – Complicated or complex

OTHER THOUGHTS

The point of this tool is to start a discussion about complexity, the challenges it throws up and the dangers of relying on transactional thinking. It may be helpful to read **Technique 10** on 'Developing your maturity in complexity'. Table 4 is a very simple table but each of the points ties back to studies on complex working. Try to avoid getting caught up in points of technical detail. The tool is designed to promote a discussion rather than to establish some form of empirical assessment.

TOOL 2 – ASSESS THE PROJECT ENVIRONMENT

PURPOSE

- To ensure that you, your team and the project sponsor go into the project with a clear and realistic view of the challenges ahead.
- To help you think about the broader systemic issues which will affect your project.

Time required: 60–120 minutes (depending upon the complexity of the project).

THE THEORY

No project exists in isolation from its environment. Success or failure is fundamentally affected by the extent to which the various systemic factors support or impede the success of the project. Systemic factors are those circumstances that can be directly influenced by the project sponsors and stakeholders. They are *systemic* in that they are based on organizational rather than personal drivers. These factors will differ with every project and so some thought is required to work out just what the critical variables might be.

It is not unusual for a project manager/team leader to find themselves sitting in front of the project sponsor after the project has started, arguing that problems have occurred due to forces outside of the team's control. This is an uncomfortable discussion because our explanations now come across as excuses. It therefore makes sense to take a pro-active approach to the potential challenge of a difficult project environment.

THE TOOL

Step 1. Organize a 'systemic review' session as early as possible in the project timeline. This will ideally involve the sponsor and a few members of the team, but it can be as few as two of you if that is appropriate.

Step 2. Pick out the key systemic variables you believe will impact on the project. These will vary according to the nature of the project and the culture of the organizations involved. Some of the more common systemic variables are set out in figure 4.

Step 3. Draw a horizontal line on a flip chart (or even just a piece of paper if there are just two of you) representing each factor. The number of factors should not exceed seven, as you need to try and keep the conversation focused.

Step 4. Ask each person present to think for a few minutes and note down their rating for each of the factors.

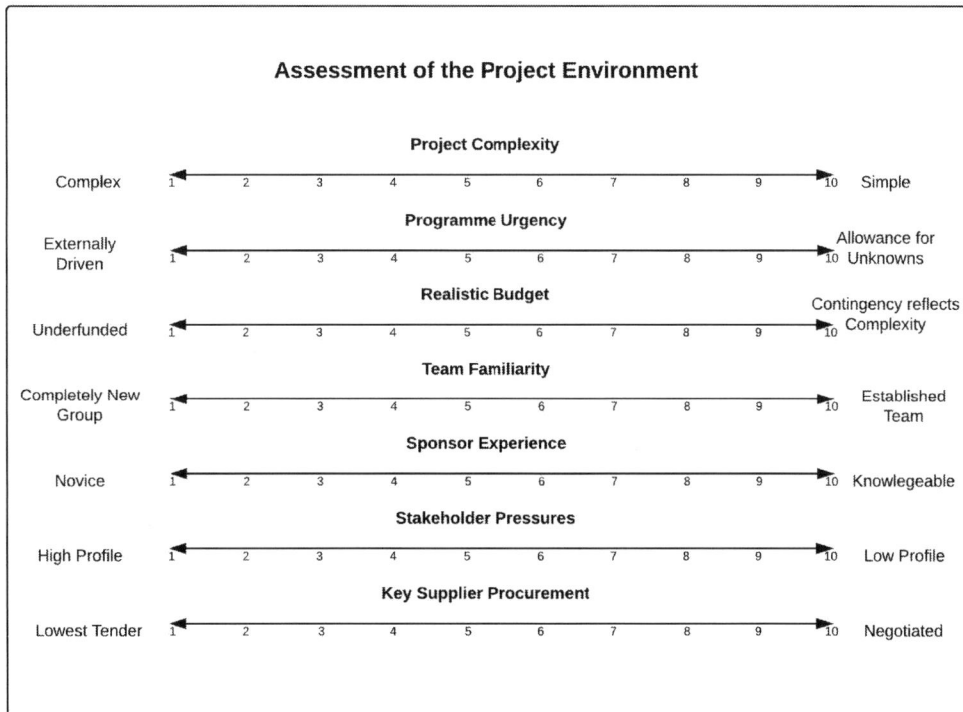

Assessment of the Project Environment

Project Complexity
Complex   1   2   3   4   5   6   7   8   9   10   Simple

Programme Urgency
Externally Driven   1   2   3   4   5   6   7   8   9   10   Allowance for Unknowns

Realistic Budget
Underfunded   1   2   3   4   5   6   7   8   9   10   Contingency reflects Complexity

Team Familiarity
Completely New Group   1   2   3   4   5   6   7   8   9   10   Established Team

Sponsor Experience
Novice   1   2   3   4   5   6   7   8   9   10   Knowlegeable

Stakeholder Pressures
High Profile   1   2   3   4   5   6   7   8   9   10   Low Profile

Key Supplier Procurement
Lowest Tender   1   2   3   4   5   6   7   8   9   10   Negotiated

Figure 4 – Assess the project environment (adapted from Llewellyn, 2015)

Step 5. Taking each of the factors in turn, ask each contributor to provide their assessment and mark their responses on the relevant continuum. You should include your own assessment as well.

Step 6. Identify where there are any significant differences in scoring and ask the question, 'How did you get to that number?'

Note: It is important not to ask 'Why do you think that?' When you ask someone 'why' you may nudge them into defending a position or point of view. This is an exercise in drawing out information, rather than engaging in debate.

OTHER THOUGHTS

Developing a greater awareness of the systemic environment could be compared to a process of stabilizing the foundations upon which the project team will work. The firmer the footing, the quicker the team will find a stable basis for working together. If the ground is soft or uneven, there is a high chance that it will create problems for the team later on. As project leader you should be going into the project with 'your eyes wide open'. If some of the environmental factors look problematic then you must acknowledge them to yourself and to the team. Don't make the common cognitive error of assuming that everything will probably be fine.

TOOL 3 – ARTICULATING STAKEHOLDER PARADOXES

PURPOSE

- To provide a mechanism for discussing paradoxical demands.
- To help the team understand stakeholder 'needs' over 'wants'.
- To enable sponsors to articulate their priorities.

Time required: 60–90 minutes.

THE THEORY

Managing complex projects, almost by definition, involves the need to manage the challenge of paradox. A paradox arises when someone makes a dual proposition that, when taken literally, is not possible to implement. Paradoxes often occur because the project environment creates a series of competing forces, which require some form of trade off. The task is to help identify, and make everyone aware of, the contradictions and inconsistencies that each stakeholder and team participant has within themselves as to what they expect the project to achieve. The most common response from team members, when faced with contradictory requirements, is to move to a position of safety and low risk. The result is a mismatch between the espoused team objectives and the reality of reduced output.

Both stakeholders and team members need to recognize the risks inherent in these paradoxes and accept a degree of compromise. If the paradoxes arising from the project environment are not acknowledged, then as team leader you open yourself to future problems. Sometimes it is simply a matter of helping separate what the sponsor really needs from the project from those features that would be 'nice to have'. More often, however, paradox arises from the competing demands of different stakeholder groups. The management of paradox requires acknowledging that there is very little that is black or white, just a series of different shades of grey. A single course of action must nevertheless be found.

THE TOOL

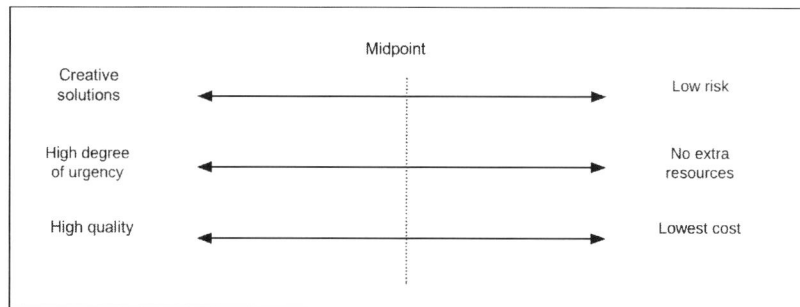

Figure 5 – Examples of typical project paradoxes (adapted from Llewellyn, 2015)

Step 1. Identify by yourself, or possibly with the wider team, any paradoxical demands being made by the sponsor or stakeholders.

Step **2.** Arrange a meeting specifically to focus on these issues. This process can be used as part of a meeting or workshop, but if there are multiple paradoxes then it is better to keep everyone focused by holding a single issue meeting.

Step **3.** Open the session by drawing up a continuum for each paradox on a flip chart or whiteboard, setting out the contrasting objectives at each end as illustrated in figure 5.

Step **4.** Describe the paradox as you see it from your perspective, explaining the practical barriers to achieving both objectives. You can take questions to clarify your explanation, but try to avoid any debate at this stage, or getting sidetracked by the detail.

Step **5.** Ask the sponsor/stakeholder to mark on the continuum where they feel the priority needs to be placed, and then *explain why*.

Step **6** You can now go into a discussion around the likely consequences of having a greater emphasis on one objective over another and how to set priorities.

OTHER THOUGHTS

This exercise is similar to the process of assessing the project environment in that it also uses a continuum to facilitate a conversation. It differs, however, in that its purpose is to map where different stakeholders' priorities lie within each paradox. It also requires asking a different set of questions to a potentially wider stakeholder group.

TOOL 4 – THE 'CUP OF TEA MEETING'

PURPOSE

- To start a dialogue with other team members before the project starts.
- To discover the personal and professional drivers of the different team members.

Time required: 90–120 minutes.

THE THEORY

There is a strong tendency in almost all project leadership teams to launch into the technical and operational challenges of a new project. The studies show, however, that there is tremendous value in spending time at the very start of a project in learning more about the people you are going to be relying on to help you deliver the project. For example, a study by Perry, Karney and Spencer (2012) looked at 26 teams of officers studying at a military academy and recorded how effectively they were able to work together over the course of a year. The study noted those teams that spent time at the start forming their goals and sharing personal experiences outperformed those that went straight into internal group process.

The thinking behind the 'cup of tea meeting' is that you instigate an informal discussion that is deliberately not technical, but instead allows you to focus on understanding what makes your new team 'tick'. This meeting is the start of your trust building process. The challenge is therefore to ensure that everyone contributes, and yet the meeting feels relaxed and unstructured.

THE TOOL

Step 1. As soon as the core team for a new project is identified, invite them to meet at a comfortable location for a 'cup of tea' (or other beverage of your choice).

Step 2. When assembled be clear this is an informal meeting whose purpose is simply to get to know each other a bit better.

Step 3. Once everyone is settled, ask each person in the group 'What are your thoughts on the new project?' This is simply a warm-up question, so don't allow the discussion to fall into a debate about technical challenges. Ensure everyone is given an opportunity to speak.

Step 4. Ask the key question 'What are your hopes and concerns about the project?' This often encourages each person to reveal some personal information without going too deeply into areas that might be uncomfortable for them.

Step 5. Finally ask each person what they hope to gain personally and professionally if/when the project is successful.

Step 6. Close the meeting by summarizing some of the key information that can be used to shape the formal kick-off workshop.

OTHER THOUGHTS

The environment that you choose is important. Everyone's voice needs to be heard, not just in the words but the nuances of pitch and tone which provide additional information. It would be wise to avoid a location where there is a lot of external noise or distraction. For this reason I would advise against holding this meeting in a pub or noisy restaurant.

CREDIT

Credit for this tool goes to Nick Fleming of Canaway Fleming Architects and his inspirational approach to leading difficult projects.

TOOL 5 – CELEBRATING CULTURAL DIVERSITY

PURPOSE

- Acknowledge issues that arise within teams from a diverse range of backgrounds and cultures
- Speed up engagement and familiarity in diverse, or multicultural teams

Time required: 60–120 minutes (depending upon the size of the team).

THE THEORY

Cultural diversity is an increasingly common feature of teams engaged in a project or initiative. Today's global cities attract a wide range of people from around the world expanding the talent pool available. The challenge for the leader of a multicultural team is to build the new group into an effective team.

Studies show that heterogeneous teams (comprising people from a diverse range of nationalities, age and gender) tend to ultimately be more productive than homogenous teams (formed from people with a similar background). Homogenous teams have the short-term advantage of being able to move into delivery mode quite quickly. They are, however, prone to 'Groupthink' (Janis, 1972) and low levels of creative challenges. Heterogeneous teams are often more creative and better at problem solving. They often, however, take more time to build the behavioural norms and communication systems needed to become an effective team.

One of the hurdles the team needs to overcome is to quickly move past the opinions and assumptions based on the cultural stereotypes that each team member has of the others. This tool is designed to stimulate conversations between team members to encourage a dialogue around the preconceptions and cultural biases that are likely to slow the creation of inter-personal trust.

THE TOOL

Step 1. Identify the potential cultural stereotypes that might exist in the team.

Step 2. Discuss your thoughts with some of your team to understand the extent to which this may or may not be an issue.

Step 3. Set up a 'communication' event. This might be a workshop or some other meeting. Explain that studies favour diverse/multicultural teams but only once they have learned to work through the communication gaps to work as a cohesive unit.

Step 4. Ask each team member to think about the cultural stereotypes that other nations might observe in them. It is important that they pick out both positive and negative attributes. Ideally these can be drawn up onto a T sheet on a flip chart or whiteboard. People from similar countries or sub-cultures might be grouped together.

Step 5. Set the ground rules. Make it clear that this should be a light-hearted exercise, and you should therefore watch for any signs that the team become too immersed in socio-cultural arguments.

Step 6. Each nationality/sub-culture then takes two minutes to explain their thoughts. Give the other members five minutes to add to or comment on each list.

Step 7. Ask the team to discuss the benefits that each culture might bring to the team.

Step 8. Ask the team to discuss what challenges might be posed by having a diverse range of cultures.

Step 9. Ask the team to discuss what steps should now be taken to get the best out of the mixed skills that are present around the table.

Step 10. Record the output and save it in the Team Integration Manual **(Tool 20)**.

OTHER THOUGHTS

The same methodology can be applied to internal teams comprising people from different departments, which are perceived to have distinct sub-cultures. If you wish to look further into this phenomenon, a good place to start is a paper by Christopher Earley and Elaine Mosakowski titled 'Creating Hybrid Team Cultures' (2000).

TOOL 6 – DANGEROUS ASSUMPTIONS AND LEAPS OF FAITH

PURPOSE

- A sense check that you are not pushing ahead without covering all of the bases.
- A simple process to guard against a conspiracy of optimism.

Time required: 15–30 minutes.

THE THEORY

It is often said that assumptions are the mother and father of all great cock-ups! Humans have a tendency to take an optimistic view as to how most projects they take on will turn out. On the whole, this is a positive attribute. If we were all pessimists, we wouldn't try anything challenging or risky. There is, however, a strong tendency to ignore peripheral or complex issues we do not understand or feel we cannot control.

We make assumptions for a number of different reasons. Often they derive from inexperience or naivety. Assumptions also provide a good example of fast, or subconscious, thinking, where we make an instinctive decision based on past experiences without fully engaging our mind on the issue.

At the start of a project or initiative, there are often many unknown factors and so we must proceed on the basis of a number of assumptions. The challenge is to be as clear as possible as to what assumptions are being made, particularly around the interactions of the people who are going to be involved in the project.

The most dangerous assumption is a 'leap of faith' which is essentially a strategy based on hope rather than statistical certainty. It is a collective, often unspoken, belief that the desired result is almost certain to happen, even though there is no evidence to support this assumption.

THE TOOL

As part of your initial planning sessions, you should ask the team to consider one or more of the following questions, depending upon the time available.

- What has to go right for this project to proceed? (Note: This is a very different question to what could go wrong.)
- What assumptions are we making about the client/sponsor?
- What assumptions are we making about the key stakeholders?
- What assumptions are we making about our ability to work as a team?
- What assumptions are we making about our resilience and how we will work when under pressure?

The final question is:

- Are we making any 'leaps of faith' here?

OTHER THOUGHTS

One of the benefits of working with a team should be the broader range of minds available to look at an issue, increasing the pool of cognitive ability to solve a problem. However, there is also a tendency towards 'Groupthink' where the team do not feel comfortable challenging any ideas that appear to have consensual support. This is often particularly a problem in homogenous teams of people who come from a similar background. This tool is an exercise that therefore benefits from taking in a mix of perspectives. Try using the 'extra chair' described in **Tool 30**, to draw out the possible views and assumptions of people who are not in the room.

The tendency towards over optimism is quite powerful, particularly if the team want the project to proceed. It is worth remembering that working on a poorly performing project is a frustrating and unrewarding experience. It is therefore better to delay or even postpone an initiative if the above reality check produces information that invites a more cautious approach.

TOOL 7 – ROLES NOT JOBS

PURPOSE

- To establish the concept that roles are distinct from job titles.
- To build flexibility into the team.
- To gain clarity as to who is accountable for what actions and outcomes.

Time required: 60 minutes.

THE THEORY

Much is written about the need for teams to have clear roles and responsibilities. In reality, people tend to focus on what they consider to be their job and approach their contribution as sitting within the constraints of their job title.

For a team assembled to deliver a project or initiative, this may not be sufficient as there are many different tasks that need to be completed on any project that sit outside the typical job description.

Roles differ from jobs in that every individual can fulfil more than one role. For example someone may have a role of technical specialist, but the project also needs them to be an ambassador (see **Tool 31**), note taker, social secretary, liaison with the finance group, team confidante, or whatever else the team needs to deliver the project.

One of the really useful aspects of roles, rather than jobs, is that roles can be interchangeable. In other words, as circumstances change you may take on new roles and pass old roles onto others. Some of these roles are informal, in that particular individuals fulfil them without any discussion. Others may require clear identification with a written explanation of the role, the outcomes expected from that role and the accountability that is attached to it.

The need for these different roles is likely to change as the project proceeds, with some roles no longer being necessary, whilst the need for new roles appears. By getting the team used to the fact that roles are not necessarily tied to their particular job description, you start to build up the flexibility that you need to adapt to changing circumstances.

THE TOOL

Step 1. Firstly look at your own personal roles in the project and be able to articulate how each one is potentially distinct.

Step 2. Introduce the concept of 'roles not jobs' to the team.

Step 3. Ask each member of the team to think for themselves for a few minutes and consider what their current different roles might be. You can use your own roles as an example, or alternatively it can be useful to use examples from home life where multiple roles are more obvious.

Step 4. Ask the team to think about the different roles that might be needed on your current project and list them out on a flip chart.

Step 5. Choose, or ask, for volunteers for any roles that are not yet allocated.

Step 6. It is now important that some work is done to set out:

- the activities/responsibilities associated with each role
- the outcomes that can be expected from the role
- the accountabilities attached to the role.

This is an iterative process, where the role description evolves, so the first pass should be a quick and dirty assessment of no more than 15 minutes for each role.

Step 7. Ask the team to swap role descriptions and see if they can be improved or need adjusting. This process is worth a couple of iterations if you have time.

OTHER THOUGHTS

Once you have role descriptions and the agreed accountability attached to that role, you are able to have much clearer conversations as to who is expected to ensure the desired outcomes are achieved. This makes it much simpler to call people to account for the contributions they have committed to.

TOOL 8 – FORCE FIELD ANALYSIS

PURPOSE

- Decision-making and problem-solving.
- A mechanism to identify and evaluate a range of issues which are likely to influence a particular outcome.

Time required: 60–90 minutes.

THE THEORY

A discussion trying to resolve an apparently complex problem or issue can quickly get bogged down in detail. In 1951 Kurt Lewin developed the concept of 'Force Field Analysis' (Lewin, 1951), which is now widely used in management contexts. Force Field Analysis works by separating the different issues surrounding a problem into 'drivers' which support movement towards a goal or objective and 'resistors' or 'blockers' that are hindering movement.

This tool is my adaptation of Lewin's concept and allows the issues to be presented visually and then scored or weighted as to their potential significance. Progress can be achieved by agreeing a series of actions that can either a) increase the strength of weak driving forces; or b) reduce the strength of strong resisting forces.

The ability to see all of the forces or factors on a single diagram helps focus the discussion, by providing a visual mechanism for articulating the relative strengths of different issues. This can often speed up the decision-making process.

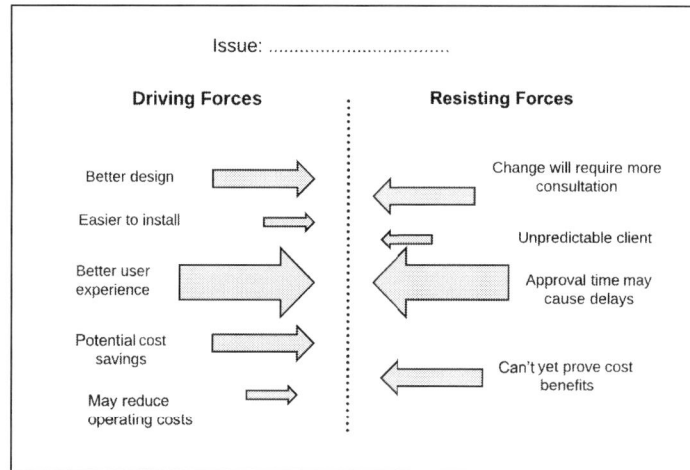

Figure 6 – An example of a Force Field Analysis

THE TOOL

Step 1. Identify the issue to be resolved.

Step 2. Set up a flip chart as in the above diagram to show the different elements as arrows.

Step 3. Identify the driving forces that are pushing towards a desired outcome.

Step 4. Identify the resisting forces that are making a decision difficult to implement.

Step 5. Ask each team member to allocate a score of between 1 and 10 to each item.

Step 6. Through discussion find an agreed score for each item.

Step 7. Ask the question 'what can we do to improve the strength of the driving forces?'

Step 8. Ask the question 'is there anything we can do to weaken the resisting forces?'

Step 9. Agree an action plan and implement.

OTHER THOUGHTS

Force Field Analysis is also a useful way of drawing out the less obvious factors that may affect a decision or solution. The analysis should therefore include some form of recognition of the systemic forces that influence a situation but are largely invisible (see **Tool 2**). It may also be useful to acknowledge the team's emotional drivers, which may be overly optimistic in a desire for the project to progress, or fears of the potential consequences of the decision to be made.

TOOL 9 – SURVIVING THE STORMING STAGE

PURPOSE

To establish your authority as team leader as the team goes through the dynamic process of settling into its behavioural norms.

Time required: Open.

THE THEORY

Many people are familiar with Bruce Tuckman's 1965 model of team dynamics in which a team makes the progression of forming, storming, norming and performing. The storming stage is a frequently observed phase which can be quite uncomfortable for the team leader.

Tuckman's observation was that when a group of people come together for the first time, their behaviour is polite and constrained as they try and work out how to react to each other. Once they become comfortable, however, they will start to test others in the group to understand the natural 'pecking order' that is likely to emerge.

The process involves a degree of chaos, or lack of order, as different people challenge both each other and the team leader to see how they react.

THE TOOL

It is not possible to accurately predict what will happen in the storming stage, or even when it will start. Much will depend upon the circumstances of the project and the personalities of the people involved. This tool is intended to help you hold a position that ensures that your authority as team leader becomes clear as the storming phase plays out. Each team will have its own circumstances and personalities, and so all you can do is be prepared. The process nevertheless involves a series of distinct activities.

Step 1. Anticipate challenge – it is useful to understand that the storming phase may be quite discrete and in some cases may not happen at all. It is important not to be surprised when your meeting agenda is thrown off course by different individuals deciding to argue about minor issues, particularly in the early meetings designed to agree task delivery.

Step 2. Be clear about roles, responsibilities and accountabilities. Ideally this is an exercise that the team has already completed **(see Tool 7)**. When the team start to squabble around seemingly minor issues, clarity of role and particularly your role as team leader provide an anchor point around which to draw a dispute to a close.

Step 3. Allow the discussions to play out. Much as you may wish to keep to your meeting agenda, if your team show a need to challenge each other, then simply focus on ensuring that any disagreement does not become personal.

Step 4. When some of your team start to challenge you, it is important to recognize that their questions or comments are unlikely to be an attack on your perceived ability to lead the group. Storming is mostly about working out who is prepared to be controlled by whom. When being challenged, simply acknowledge the questions or statements, and *respond in the context of the role of the leader.* Keep in mind that in this early stage, you do not need to fix other people's problems, or satisfy their individual demands. Your role is to deliver the project outcome and your team will eventually settle into a set of collectively understood behavioural norms and can now start delivering the task for which they have been assembled.

OTHER THOUGHTS

The storming stage may be worked through over the course of a team meeting. It may, however, take place over a period of weeks. When the stage is prolonged, you may start to feel that there is a lack of belief in your leadership, which can easily erode your self-confidence. Try not to take this disruption personally. You must remain patient and wait until the process has worked its way out and the team move into the 'norming' phase.

Chapter 5

TOOLS FOR SETTING UP AN EFFECTIVE TEAM

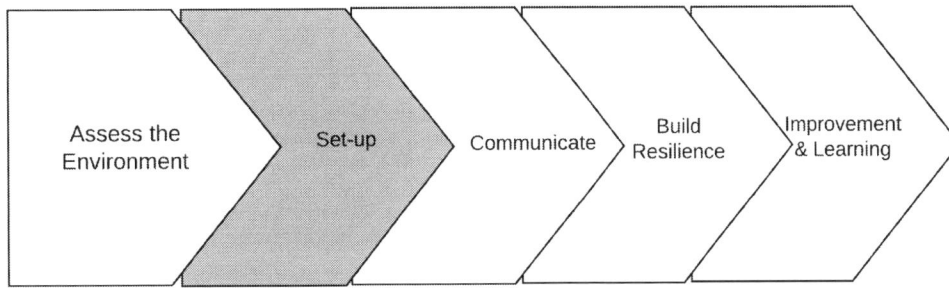

Figure 2B – Team coaching model: Set-up

Tool 10	The Big 'Why?'
Tool 11	Extrovert and introvert thinking
Tool 12	Learning from the past
Tool 13	Establishing your rules of engagement
Tool 14	Taking feedback
Tool 15	Building the future story
Tool 16	How to motivate or annoy me
Tool 17	The collaboration canvas
Tool 18	Create an awareness of behavioural gravity
Tool 19	Establish a 'no blame' culture
Tool 20	The Team Integration Manual

TOOL 10 – THE BIG 'WHY?'

PURPOSE

- To build motivation and the commitment of the team members to your project.
- To provide a focal point for future decision-making.
- To establish connections with the project's stakeholders.

Time required: 15–45 minutes.

THE THEORY

Every expert on team performance agrees that teams need some form of vision that will bind them together in their endeavour. According to Michael West (2011) 'Vision is a shared idea of a valued outcome which provides motivation for the team's work'. Your objective as team leader is to help each member connect their own intrinsic motivations with the outcome of the project. The key insight is to recognize that individuals may have different factors that motivate them. Their drivers might include:

- personal success
- being part of a great team
- making a contribution to society
- a step forward in their career
- a new learning experience
- professional pride.

It is therefore important to draw out these motivational factors, not only to bring them into individual consciousness, but also to ensure that each team member understands what motivates others in the group.

THE TOOL

Step 1. Include 'Vision for the Project' as an early item for discussion in your set-up workshop, allowing space in the agenda for a full group discussion.

Step 2. At the meeting/workshop explain the importance of having a common vision for the project so that everyone is working to a common purpose, including the recognition that each person will have their own particular motivational drivers.

Step 3. Articulate the client's/sponsor's vision for the project. Where possible, ask the client to join the meeting to explain the economic and social drivers that sit behind the project. Having a sponsor who is passionate about the project speak to the group can have a powerful impact on their motivation. The purpose of this step is to help the team visualize what will happen when the project outcomes are successful. If the sponsor is not available, then you, or another member of the team, will have to speak on their behalf. Ask the team if they have any clarifying questions or comments.

Step 4. Explain again that everyone around the table is likely to have different motivational drivers. Possibly run through the bullet points above to illustrate your point. Then ask the team to write down, 'what would a successful outcome on this project look like for you, and what would it do for you, both personally and professionally?'

Step 5. Ask each team member to speak for up to, but no more than, three minutes. It is crucial that each person is allowed to talk with no interruption. Allow the others to ask for clarification, but there should be no comments or discussion until after each person has spoken. It is important that all the contributions are made sequentially. This may well be one of the first opportunities you have to encourage team members to reveal something about their personality, so it is important that they feel that everyone has listened to them speak. Ideally start with one or two team members who you know are enthusiastic about the project. This will help adjust the mindset of the others in the room.

(Whoever is facilitating may want to pick out some of the key factors for each person on a flip chart, or whiteboard, but this is optional. Sometimes it is better to make this part of a workshop feel informal.)

Step 6. Close the session simply by asking the group how they currently *feel* about the project? The responses will give you some idea of the extent to which you have stimulated a degree of emotional energy, which will establish a deeper commitment to the success of the project.

OTHER THOUGHTS

1. This tool works very well in a project set-up workshop but could also work as a stand-alone exercise. An alternative exercise for smaller teams is the '*cup of tea meeting*' as described in **Tool 4.**

2. It is possible that some team members may be initially unwilling to reveal any personal information, and you may get a response along the lines of

    'I am just here for the money'

    'It's my job'

    'I am here because I was told to be'.

    Such responses are an important indicator of the type of team that is likely to develop and so it is worth exploring further. For younger team members who appear uncomfortable with the question you might gently enquire, 'So why did you become an engineer/ designer/ manager/ technician etc?' or 'if this project is successful, do you think it will improve your career prospects?'

3. From others you may occasionally detect a more cynical response, particularly from an experienced member of the group. This may be a subtle challenge to your authority as leader, so take it as a signal, but do not react to the challenge as part of this exercise. Just confirm that you heard what they said and move on to the next team member. You can then decide how to react to the challenge at a later stage. (**See Tool 9** – Surviving the storming stage.)

TOOL 11 – EXTROVERT AND INTROVERT THINKING

PURPOSE

- To gain the full participation of the team.
- To reduce the impact of dominant personalities taking over a meeting.
- To improve awareness.
- To build trust.

Time required: 15–30 minutes depending upon the size of the team.

THE THEORY

When expressing our thoughts, all humans sit on a continuum. At one end are people who find it easier to firm up their thoughts as they speak them out loud. As ideas come to them, they talk to find the words to articulate their point of view. Such people are referred to as *extrovert thinkers*. This does not mean that they cannot think quietly by themselves, but when they become excited they have a strong urge to speak, often interrupting others who may also be trying to form their own thoughts.

At the other end of the continuum are *introverted thinkers*. These are people who like to think things through by themselves. They do not necessarily need to involve others. Having worked through an issue, they will come to a conclusion, but will not necessarily feel any need to explain their thinking to the others around the table.

We all sit somewhere on this continuum, and most people will sit close to the centre sometimes switching between introversion and extroversion. A proportion of the population will, however, sit towards either end of the line. People with strong introvert or extrovert tendencies are often unaware of the effect they have on a discussion. Meetings are likely to be more effective if extroverts are reminded to hold their urge to interrupt, and introverts are encouraged to add their thinking to the discussion. The purpose of the tool is to help each member of the team consider their preference/habit and to also observe the tendencies in others.

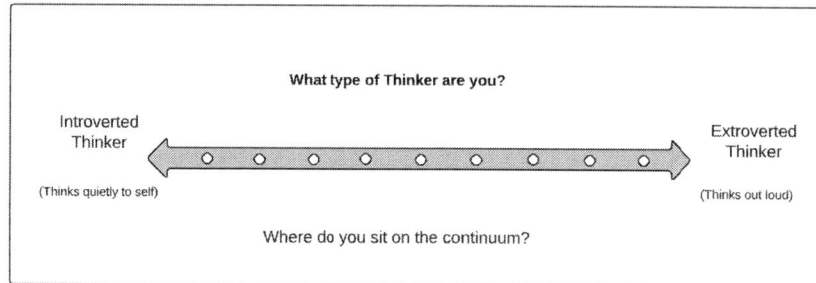

Figure 7 – Introvert–extrovert continuum

THE TOOL

Step 1. Explain the theory as outlined above.

Step 2. Draw a line on a flip chart or whiteboard as shown in figure 7.

Step 3. Ask each team member to identify for themselves where they might fit on the continuum but to keep their position to themselves for the moment.

Step 4. If the team have already spent some time together, ask the team to assess each other, and see what emerges from the discussion. If you are working with a new team, simply ask them to try and identify where they sit on the continuum.

Step 5. Ask the team what they feel they have learned from the exercise and how this information should be used to improve future team meetings.

OTHER THOUGHTS

Using the continuum helps keep the conversation focused on the issue, which can otherwise spiral off into different series of topics. By allowing each person to mark up their position on the line, you also provide a visual touch point that will help you draw the conversation back to the original question.

TOOL 12 – LEARNING FROM THE PAST

PURPOSE

To bring the learning from the team's experiences of past projects into your new project.

Time required: 30–60 minutes.

THE THEORY

When the team comes together formally for the first time or in a set-up workshop, it is useful to try and bring in some of their experiences from the past. Using stories from past projects engages the interest of others in the room and allows each member of the team to talk about something they have learned that is likely to be useful to the team's current initiative.

The value of using stories is that they provide context to the lessons that have been learned, without imposing a direct proposal as to what the team should or should not do with that information. By capturing the key points from the stories you can nevertheless start to build a number of actions that begin the process of shaping your team's attitude and approach.

THE TOOL

Step 1. Ask them to think for a couple of minutes of a project or past experience which either went really well or really badly. Ask them to make some brief notes. Be clear that you are looking for a mix of good and bad experience.

Step 2. Depending upon how many people there are in the room split the team into pairs or groups of three or four.

Step 3. Ask the team to tell their story to others in their group. Allow three to five minutes for each person.

Step 4. Ask the group to write on a big piece of paper or a flip chart what lessons from the past might be useful to the current team.

Step 5. Ask each group to present one or two of their stories to the room, illustrating the points drawn up on their flip chart/paper.

Step 6. Capture a summary of the key points.

Step 7. Picking out a number of the most pertinent points, lead a discussion as to how these lessons could be incorporated into the team's working practices.

Step 8. Use the output from this discussion to inform your rules of engagement/team charter (see **Tool 13**).

OTHER THOUGHTS

As discussed in **Technique 8**, stories are a very effective mechanism for passing on learning. These stories of what happened in the past will resonate more strongly than showing the team a PowerPoint slide of good and bad team process. So whilst this exercise may at first glance appear simplistic it is worth giving the exercise the time it needs to play out.

TOOL 13 – ESTABLISHING YOUR RULES OF ENGAGEMENT

PURPOSE

- To establish protocols for team meetings.
- To encourage positive communication.
- To discourage destructive meeting behaviours.

Time required: 15–30 minutes.

THE THEORY

When a team formally comes together for the first time, there is an opportunity to establish a new set of behaviours particularly around meetings. In a new group, humans are prepared to adapt their behaviour to the norms of that group. There is a 'one shot' opportunity to establish effective meeting behaviours, which only occurs in the early part of a team's existence. In the absence of specific agreement, however, group norms will default to the behaviours that were deemed satisfactory in previous teams or projects. The following process allows you to introduce a clear set of rules of engagement without appearing to dictate your own personal expectations. The rules that emerge *must come from the group* so that they become the team's rules, not yours. Human beings are much more likely to adopt rules which they feel they have had a role in drafting. On the other hand, if rules are imposed upon us, we will often devote a disproportionate amount of energy to trying to subtly subvert them.

THE TOOL

Step 1. Ask each of the team to think of a meeting from a previous project that was either effective or ineffective.

Step 2. Draw up a T chart as illustrated in figure 7. (Alternatively use two flip charts if they are available.)

Step 3. Ask the team to call out both positive and negative behaviours they have experienced in previous teams and write them onto the chart.

Step 4. After filling the chart, ask the team to now identify which of the examples could be adopted for the new project or initiative, and which should be avoided.

Step 5. Start to draw up a rough document, ideally on a new sheet of flip chart paper, so that the team can see the rules they are co-creating. (This can be tidied up into a more formal document later if necessary.)

Good Meeting	Bad Meeting
Clear agenda	Some people arriving late
Start and finish on time	Confused messages/actions
Well chaired	Issues keep coming back without resolution
People come prepared	Inappropriate notes
Meeting is relevant	Bad behaviours such as talking over one another, looking at email on the phone and leaving early without notice
Minutes written up quikly	
The right people attend	
Able to make decisions	Meeting is unnecessary
Where possible involve cake!	Not enough cake!

Figure 8 – Illustration of good meeting/bad meeting exercise

Step 6. Ask each individual member of the team whether they are prepared to sign up to the document that will effectively govern behaviours in all future team meetings.

Step 7. Within 48 hours circulate a document that sets out the agreed 'Rules of Engagement' for this project, and incorporate it into the Team Integration Manual.

OTHER THOUGHTS

1. This exercise can become confused with the creation of a 'team charter'. My reservation around team charters is that the concept has become distorted to include a range of information that has little to do with influencing behaviours. They are often pre-written, negating the fundamental value in having a co-created document into which everyone has had an input.
2. The exercise can be usefully extended to also incorporate how the team will communicate outside of team meetings.
3. See also **Tool 28** – 'Agree your meeting strategy'.

TOOL 14 – AGREEING TO TAKE FEEDBACK

PURPOSE

- To prepare the team to be open to giving and receiving feedback about the team's performance.
- To make it easier to implement a feedback process once the project is underway.
- To agree how and when the feedback process will work.

Time required: 45–60 minutes.

THE THEORY

Having a system for obtaining and then absorbing clear feedback has consistently been found to be an essential component in the creation and maintenance of an effective team.

Feedback provides the critical information that a team needs to:

- develop its communication and collaborative skills
- identify process that is not working
- provide positive reinforcement of positive team attributes
- create an opportunity to correct negative behaviours affecting team performance, and
- identify and adapt to changing circumstances.

The problem most teams face is that professionals tend to dislike any feedback that might be perceived to be critical of their work or their personality. Consequently, few teams plan any form of feedback process into the programme. It then becomes much more difficult to introduce a feedback system once the project is underway.

The purpose of this exercise is to start a discussion on the need for feedback and how the process they choose will work. A detailed explanation of potential feedback mechanisms is provided as a separate tool (see **Tool 42**).

THE TOOL

Step 1. Introduce the question of taking feedback into the agenda of an early team meeting. This matter does not necessarily need to take up time in the start-up meeting, but should be discussed before the project gets fully underway.

Step 2. Introduce the concept of team feedback as a process setting out the five key benefits outlined above.

Step 3. Ask the team to say how they feel about the idea of having a feedback process. Each team member should be allowed to have their say without interruption. Avoid getting into the detail of how the feedback process will work at this stage. You are primarily seeking a consensus that the principle of taking team feedback will be useful.

Step 4. On the assumption that you get agreement in principle*, you can now proceed into a discussion as to what type of feedback process is likely to be most suited and practical for the needs of the team. There are a wide range of proprietary feedback tools available, some provided as a consultancy package, others as online facilities. It is also perfectly feasible to create your own process.

Step 5. You can explain that there are essentially two different approaches to gaining feedback. The first is to use a self-managed process where the team undertakes a review of itself. The other is where the team takes information from outside the team in the form of a 360-degree assessment. In simple terms the advantages and disadvantages of each are summarized in table 5.

Feedback Approach	Advantages	Disadvantages
1. Internal to the team, where data is only collected from team members	Quick and relatively easy. Can be verbal or based on a bespoke questionnaire	Feedback may be too introspective, without seeing the wider context. Easy to avoid the difficult issues
2. External 360, where data is collected from stakeholders, subordinates and suppliers	Wider data source provides more objective information. Also allows the team to see the project from a different perspective	External input needs time and resource to administer. May need third party to analyse, anonymize and report the data

Table 5 – Alternative approaches to gaining feedback

Step 6. Once you have agreed the type of feedback tool you are going to use, you then need to agree at what stages in the project cycle you will take feedback, and how the data will be presented to the team.

* Note: If you do not get agreement from the team to take feedback, this is a significant 'red flag' that some, or all, of the members do not yet feel they are in a psychologically safe environment. Left unchecked, this is a portent of problems ahead.

TOOL 15 – BUILDING A FUTURE STORY

PURPOSE

- To embed the vision for the project.
- To articulate the team's mission.
- To set a positive mindset on what is going to be achieved.

Time required: 60 minutes.

THE THEORY

This is a positive exercise designed to help the team develop a forward-looking mindset focused on success. The tool works well as part of a kick-off workshop.

Stories are a simple but powerful mechanism for helping humans make sense of a complex situation. We also remember stories much more easily than we can recall facts and figures. Creating a story of what is going to happen nudges the team to think about a point in the future when the project is complete and obstacles have been overcome and the sponsors and

EXAMPLE OF A FUTURE STORY

'Today, we finally handed over the completed documentation to the engineering team. This has been a really satisfying and enjoyable project to work on. It has been very challenging at times, but the collaborative spirit that was created in the team from the very start has helped us succeed. By investing in the right behaviours we were able to establish an open and transparent culture which encouraged innovation and creative thinking.

'It has helped having a clear vision of what we were trying to achieve, and the importance that the project is likely to have to future generations of people around the world. At the start, we set up a clear governance structure and every member of the team knew both their role and what they were going to be accountable for. That said it was great to users are delighted with the outcome. It is a form of self-fulfilling prophecy.

THE TOOL

Step 1. Explain the concept of future visioning. Ask the team to imagine a day in the future shortly after the project has been completed. An article has been written which talks about the project.

Step 2. On a flip chart/whiteboard write 'what does the article say about the project?'

Step 3. What does it say about how the users feel about the outcome?

Step 4. What does it say about the challenges the team had to overcome?

Step 5. Pull the different elements together into a single statement. An example might look like the text in the box.

Step 6. Write up and circulate this statement as part of the Team Integration Manual.

Note: This exercise builds on the vision exercise set out in **Tool 10**. It does not replace it.

see how the team supported each other when the pressure was on. We managed to establish a genuine "no blame" culture so that the team learned from the experiences as the project progressed.

'The external contractors were carefully selected to ensure that we maintained the collaborative team ethos through the transition from design to delivery. Using regular workshops we were able to be flexible in our thinking and adaptable in our approach. So despite the challenges of working through complex and changing external conditions, we have delivered the project within budget and on time.

'Wherever possible we kept the numerous stakeholder groups engaged and connected to the programme, and actively sought feedback from within the wider organization to ensure that we were adapting to the needs of the project. The result is a comprehensive set of documentation that we are all so proud to have helped create.'

TOOL 16 – HOW TO MOTIVATE OR ANNOY ME

PURPOSE

- To help team members understand what motivates them and what annoys them.
- To improve communications within the team.
- To gain some additional clues about your team's motivations and preferences.

Time required: 45–60 minutes.

THE THEORY

When a team first comes together they tend to focus on the technical challenge. They often do not get to know each other's drivers until they have worked together for a period of time (if at all).

It is important to recognize that what motivates one team member may irritate or offend another. It is difficult to quickly tell, however, what each person's 'hot buttons' are, just by working alongside them. Unless of course you ask.

THE TOOL

Step 1. Provide every member of the team with a large sheet of paper. This could be flip chart paper or even space on a whiteboard. The purpose of the exercise is to write in sufficiently large font that they can present back to the rest of the room.

Step 2. Ask the team to divide their paper into four sections.

Step 3. Ask the team to label the four quadrants as illustrated in figure 9.

I work well when…	If you want to motivate me…
Work is hard when…	If you want to annoy me…

Figure 9 – Set up for the motivate or annoy me exercise

Step 4. Ask each member of the team to spend 10 minutes filling in their personal views on each point. Encourage them to identify two or more points under each heading.

Step 5. Having had time to put their thoughts on paper, ask them to post their paper on a suitable wall surface where these thoughts can be seen by the others. (You may need some Blu tack or similar temporary method of sticking the paper up.)

Step 6. Ask each team member in turn to explain to the others in the room what they have written under each heading. Allow two to three minutes for each person. Everyone speaks and everyone listens.

Step 7. Ask the team what they have learned from the exercise and what they might use this information for in the future.

Step 8. Once everyone has spoken gather the papers together and later compile them into a single document that can be circulated.

OTHER THOUGHTS

1. This is a simple exercise designed to get your team to start to reveal a bit about their personal preferences and motivations. Try not to allow it to be overcomplicated. If possible, have a bit of fun with it.
2. The tool provides a great exercise to use at the start of a workshop or a team away day.
3. Three or four months after the exercise was first done circulate the results at a team meeting to remind team members of what was said and ask if anyone would add or change anything. Then point out the benefits of understanding the different drivers within the team.

CREDIT

My thanks to my good friend Will Karlsen for introducing me to this tool at one of his thoroughly engaging experiential workshops.

TOOL 17 – THE COLLABORATION CANVAS

PURPOSE

To provide a structure and format for a set-up workshop or meeting intended to establish the right behavioural norms.

Time required: 30 minutes (preparation time).

THE THEORY

Designing a project set-up or initiation workshop can become complicated, particularly if the time available has become compressed. There are many areas that might be covered in the agenda, and so there is a danger that insufficient time is allocated to each of the key areas.

The collaboration canvas is a workshop tool used as part the project set-up process. Its purpose is to help the team agree a plan of action to embed collaborative behaviours throughout the project. The canvas comprises a number of boxes set out in three by three matrix, with pre-printed headings in each of the boxes. Each heading covers one of the key elements found to be essential in establishing strong behavioural norms. The sheet is printed off in large print size (A0 or A1) for use in the workshop. The team then use the canvas both as a visual agenda for items to be discussed, and then to provide a record of the actions agreed in the workshop.

The visual display can be very useful in helping the team to see the bigger picture around the development of the team, and the need to pay attention to each of the aspects to be covered. The canvas encourages the team to take time to fill in all of the boxes. White space left unfilled is a reminder that the set-up process is incomplete.

A generic example which covers the key areas of team set-up for most projects is illustrated in figure 10. These headings are derived from the studies on team performance. However, you may have different needs and so you can simply use whatever headings are most useful to your event.

You can download a copy of this diagram at www.teamcoachingtoolkit.com/the-collaboration-canvas/

Assess The Project Environment	The Big 'Why'	Stakeholders and Ambassadors
Key Roles and Responsibilities	Our Vision and Values	Our Rules of Engagement
Building in Resilience	Our Learning Strategy	Outstanding Actions

Figure 10 – An example of a collaboration canvas

THE TOOL

Step 1. Review the example shown in figure 10 and decide which headings you wish to use in your workshop. You may, however, wish to adapt the headings to suit the current status of your project.

Step 2. Design your own version of the canvas or download a copy from the website.

Step 3. Arrange for a large copy to be printed. If you have access to a plotter this should make it easier, but large size prints can also be created by most high street print agencies.

Step 4. Place the paper up on the wall so that it provides a visual agenda for the team to work through. As key issues are discussed and actions agreed write a summary in the relevant box.

Step 5. Once the meeting has finished, appoint someone to adapt the content on the canvas in to the 'Team Integration Manual' (see **Tool 20**)

OTHER THOUGHTS

You do not need to be tied to the 3 x 3 format. Once you know how many areas you want to cover in the session, simply design the canvas to create enough boxes to ensure that you touch all of the elements of your plan.

This tool can work very well if you are working with a large group. I have used it very successfully at a conference of 60 project managers and consultants, where we split the room into a number of sub-teams who then worked on a series of different canvasses. The output was then pulled together to establish a set of best practice procedures for setting up their projects.

TOOL 18 – CREATE AN AWARENESS OF BEHAVIOURAL GRAVITY

PURPOSE

To build an awareness in the team of the need to spend time and energy to develop trust and strong behavioural norms.

Time required: 10–15 minutes.

THE THEORY

Whilst most human beings are genetically programmed to work in groups we have a remarkable ability to fall out with each other. When a new team forms the members come together as a group who have yet to learn to trust each other. If active steps are not taken then as the individuals start to work together they will often find reasons to disagree and eventually fall into conflict.

Many teams suffer from a false assumption that everyone will behave rationally and logically according to their own particular version as to what is rational or logical. There is sometimes a degree of resistance to the prospect of investing in the team development activities set out in this toolkit, only to find out too late that the team has established a set of dysfunctional behavioural norms.

The diagram below provides a simple mechanism to explain the challenge of 'behavioural gravity' (Llewellyn, 2015) and why it is essential to put some time into the activities that are found to build trust and maintain cohesion.

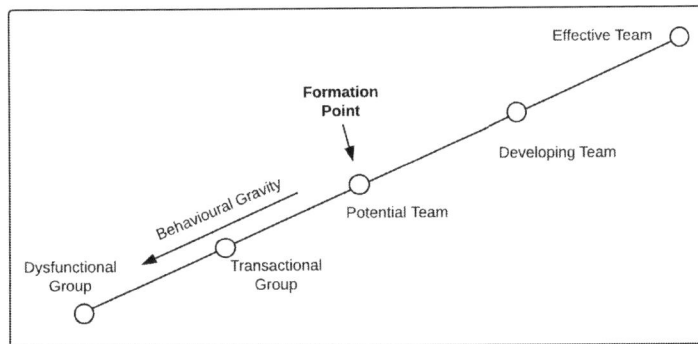

Figure 11 – Illustration of behavioural gravity (adapted from Llewellyn, 2015)

THE TOOL

Step 1. Ask your new team to think about a previous experience in a team or group where the behaviours were good or bad. If time is available have a discussion but if you are on a tight programme move to Step 2.

Step 2. Draw the above diagram onto a flip chart or whiteboard.

Step 3. Explain the conceptual idea that you have all come together on the side of a hill. Ask how comfortable it is to try and stand for any time on sloping ground.

Step 4. Explain that the dark side of human nature pulls us towards dysfunctional behaviours arising from poor communication, low levels of trust and ultimately disengagement.

Step 5. Explain that if the team wishes to become a cohesive unit then they need to do those things that will help them move up the slope towards the position where they can become a strong team.

Step 6. Explain the selection of activities you feel will help the team work against Behavioural Gravity and ask what they think about your proposal.

OTHER THOUGHTS

I was once involved in a set-up meeting for a complex relocation project. The senior managers present were impatient to press on with planning the programme, and were resistant to spending any time establishing the collaborative norms that were going to be needed to make the project work. There was an assumption in the room that since everyone was behaving rationally, this would continue into the period when the group would be under pressure. Using the above diagram, I was able to ask them to reflect on their previous experiences in both good and bad teams. The idea of gravity pulling them towards dysfunctional relationships made sufficient sense for them to agree to slow down and spend some time thinking about how they were going to work together as a real team.

TOOL 19 – ESTABLISH A 'NO BLAME' CULTURE

PURPOSE

- To ensure the team understand the benefits of creating a blame free environment.
- To establish the principle of emotional self-control.

Time required: 30 minutes.

THE THEORY

Humans have an instinctive need to apportion blame when something does not go according to plan. The desire to blame comes from a range of emotional reactions such as anger, fear, disgust, sadness and surprise. These are 'avoidance' emotions that are programmed into our genetic structure to aid survival. When an unpleasant or undesirable event occurs our bodies push out chemicals which generate feelings that are initially out of our control. The feel-think-act response means that we have to learn to recognize a natural instinct to find someone upon whom we can focus our negative feelings. Once we are aware this is an instinctive reaction, we can then manage our emotions and start to adopt a rational response.

The downside of seeking to blame someone else is that that passes control of any potential solution over to another party. This can be particularly problematic for a team who finds itself continually blaming external stakeholders for problems which then detracts from their ability to find their own solutions. By continually looking at a problem and asking yourselves, how can we sort this, you retain the ability to move forward, without the emotional baggage that will otherwise slow the team's progress.

I regularly come across many teams who claim to want to work in a 'no blame' culture but do not know how to make it work. Figure 12 sets out a simple procedure.

No Blame Protocol

1. Acknowledge your emotional reactions to the event and then park them aside.

2. Now focus on the facts and seek to dispassionately understand what has happened and why.

3. Where appropriate, talk about the situation openly with those involved, using dialogue rather than accusation.

4. Consider the options available to rectify the situation.

5. Ask yourself and the others in the team what has been learned from the situation.

6. Agree whatever changes are needed in the team's process to prevent a similar occurance.

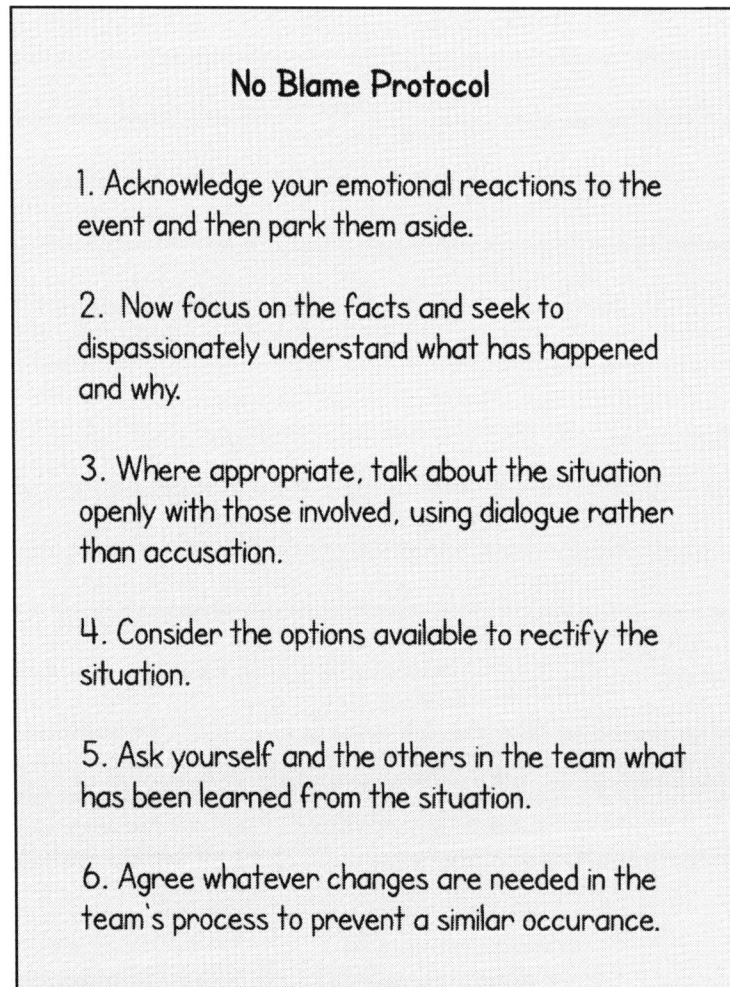

Figure 12 – 'No blame' protocol

THE TOOL

Step 1. Stimulate an early discussion specifically to talk about what 'no blame' culture actually means.

Step 2. Ask the team what they think a 'no blame' culture looks like. Write up any key points to create a point of focus.

Step 3. Explain the challenge of feel-think-act and the need to recognize the emotional urge to find fault in others.

Step 4. Ask for examples of situations that might apply to the team where no blame should be attributed.

Step 5. Ask how 'no blame' sits with accountability and the need to deliver on commitments.

Step 6. Suggest the team adapt and then adopt the 'no blame' protocol set out in figure 12.

Step 7. As soon as the first major problem arises it is essential to revisit your no blame protocol and test it out. It is this first iteration that will govern whether the team can truly adopt a 'no blame' culture.

OTHER THOUGHTS

One of the problems with blame is that it tends to be circular. It is quite common to find a situation where one person (or part of the organization) does not finish her contribution on time, forcing the team to miss an important deadline. When quizzed, she complains that it was not her fault because another part of the team did not give her the data when it was promised. The explanation then provided by this third link in the enquiry is that he was not given enough time by his manager, and was then pulled onto another project. It is surprising how often the loop ends back with the sponsor or project manager for not taking some action earlier in the project timeline. I have seen this happen in teams of all shapes and sizes. The teams who manage to move quickly through the no blame protocol are much more able to learn from the problem and become more effective. Those that do not tend to struggle to maintain good communication, and relationships start to become dysfunctional.

TOOL 20 – THE TEAM INTEGRATION MANUAL

PURPOSE

- To establish and then build a repository for all the information created by the team that relates to the activities and behaviours needed to maintain team effectiveness.
- To create an important induction tool for new members joining the team after its inception.

Time required: 60 minutes to set up and then regular maintenance thereafter.

THE THEORY

If you follow the model of team coaching set out in this book, you will have invested time early in the project cycle, setting in motion a number of activities that will generate actions and protocols agreed by the team. All of this good work will have been wasted if you do not ensure that these agreed outcomes are then implemented. As the team moves into task completion, it is easy to forget the early work designed to establish strong team behaviours, and bad habits can develop. Part of the coaching solution is to create a 'Team Integration Manual'. This is essentially a folder containing all of the outputs from the various activities, discussions and other exercises that are part of the set-up process.

To have an impact the manual must be regarded as one of the key tools used by the team as they work towards their objective. The folder must be regarded as a set of live documents, which are regularly referenced, and are kept up-to-date. The folder then also becomes a primary element in the induction process for new additions to the team, setting out in clear terms, '*This is how we do things in this team.*'

Examples of the types of document that the Team Integration Manual will include are set out below.

- The team's vision, mission and values (**Tool 10**).

- The key roles, responsibilities and accountabilities that have been agreed by the team (**Tool 9**).
- The stakeholder engagement plan (**Tool 31**).
- The team's 'rules of engagement' (**Tool 13**).
- The team's future story (**Tool 15**).
- The team's psychometric profile (**Tool 23**).
- What motivates and demotivates individual team members (**Tool 16**).
- Areas of specific complexity (**Tool 1**).
- Output from the meetings of the collaboration and integration group (**Tool 21**).
- Output from the periodic feedback exercises (**Tool 42**).
- The agreed mechanism for undertaking regular 'learning and reflection' sessions (**Tool 44**).

This is not a comprehensive list as there are likely to be other documents that are specific to your project or team.

THE TOOL

Step 1. Nominate someone from the team to take on the role of ownership of the Team Integration Manual. Ownership is critical to the tool's effectiveness, and so this role must be regarded by the whole team as an important responsibility.

Step 2. Decide on the format in which the manual will exist. Is it a hard copy, which is kept in the team's primary location, or, alternatively, copied and distributed to each individual? Alternatively, you may decide to keep the manual in soft form, to be held on a shared technology platform.

Step 3. Establish the manual as part of the team's governance and on-boarding process.

OTHER THOUGHTS

Establishing the use of this tool in the early stages of the team's existence will give you a great return on any time taken to set it up. Try not to look at the process as optional. Putting a priority on the collection and curation of this information sends a signal to the team that collaborative behaviours are a critical element of the team's culture.

CHAPTER 6

TOOLS FOR IMPROVING COMMUNICATION

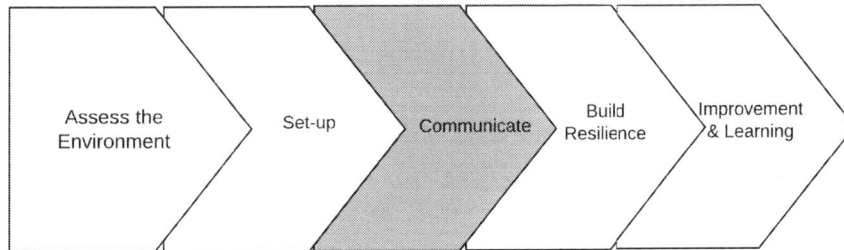

```
Assess the          Set-up    Communicate    Build      Improvement
Environment                                 Resilience   & Learning
```

Figure 2C – Team coaching model: Communicate

Tool 21	Establish a collaboration and integration workstream
Tool 22	The language of collaboration
Tool 23	Building a team psychometric profile
Tool 24	Everyone speaks and everyone is heard
Tool 25	Systemic problem-solving model
Tool 26	Who plays the fool?
Tool 27	The 'so what?' monitor
Tool 28	Agree your meeting strategy
Tool 29	Identifying the elephant
Tool 30	Perceptual positions from the 'extra chair'
Tool 31	Building stakeholder support

TOOL 21 – ESTABLISH A COLLABORATION AND INTEGRATION WORKSTREAM

PURPOSE

To establish a separate workstream involving a group of senior individuals who take on the role of ensuring the relevant actions are taken to ensure the team form an effective and cohesive unit.

Time required: Ongoing throughout the team's life cycle.

THE THEORY/TOOL

There is an overwhelming tendency in teams to focus almost exclusively on the task completion. On projects that require the effective integration of a large number of people it is useful to establish a separate workstream with the distinct remit to focus on *how* the team will work together rather than on *what* it does.

By giving this workstream a name, such as the Collaboration and Integration Group (CIG), you create an identity that is understood by the wider team. The CIG (or whatever name you choose) must manage an ongoing agenda that will deal with the more problematic issues that

CASE STORY

To give an example, I have a case story of a joint venture between two large organizations who won a contract to deliver a complex communication infrastructure project. The senior managers from both organizations had the sense to recognize that the joint venture would not achieve the stretching targets they had been set unless they worked together as a single team. They therefore set up a small group of managers whose role was to run a workstream which they called 'One Team'. This group now had a specific remit to find different mechanisms to build a one team ethos. Some of their actions included rebranding the team as a distinct unit rather than as an amalgam of the parent companies, putting in place a thorough induction process to embed collaborative behaviours and deliberately creating a behavioural culture arise around relationships and building posi-tive social interconnections with people in and around the project or initiative.

The CIG remit would include activities such as:

specific to that project. As the project progressed, they used regular feedback on a number of key measures to mon-itor the attitudes of the team and the extent to which they avoided falling into tribal behaviours when under pressure.

- commissioning a team development and project initiation workshop
- establishing behavioural key performance indicators and commissioning systems to manage them
- taking ownership for the creation and maintenance of the Team Integration Manual (see **Tool 20**)
- commissioning the design and implementation of a feedback system (see **Tool 42**)
- receiving and discussing feedback reports and recommending action
- instigating regular team learning and reflection sessions (see **Tools 39, 40 and 44**)
- monitoring the collective resilience of the team and the extent that parts of the team are able to manage periods of pressure and stress.

To be effective the CIG must comprise a number of senior individuals who have the authority to make decision on the team's behalf and implement them without becoming stuck in a hier-archical decision-making process.

TOOL 22 – THE LANGUAGE OF COLLABORATION

PURPOSE

- To build awareness of the problems caused by instinctive language.
- To equip the team with the habits of open communication.

Time required: 45–60 minutes.

THE THEORY

Clear and open communication sits at the heart of an effectively functioning team. How the members speak to each other will fundamentally affect the speed with which they learn to trust each other. To become a cohesive unit, teams must build the confidence to explore new ideas and to deal with difficult issues. Unfortunately many professionals have learned speech patterns that are more likely to close down communication, using the language of control rather than the more neutral style that is needed for collaboration. The exercise below is designed to help the team develop a greater awareness of the impact of speech patterns and to agree their own plans to try and work together to promote collaborative language.

Language of Enquiry		Language of Control
Dialogue	versus	Debate
Influence	versus	Coercion
Clarity	versus	Ambiguity
Assertive	versus	Aggressive
Open	versus	Closed
Steering	versus	Driving

Figure 13 – Enquiring versus controlling language styles

THE TOOL

STAGE 1

Step 1. Figure 13 above sets out a number of parameters that illustrate collaborative speech patterns as opposed to controlling patterns. Draw the table up onto a flip chart.

Step 2. Organize the team into pairs and allocate one set of parameters to each. Each group ideally has a piece of flip chart paper or whiteboard space to write on. For example, what are the types of language that you would associate with dialogue and how are they different from the words and phrases used in debate?

Step 3. Ask the groups to spend 10 minutes thinking of as many examples as they can of *controlling* versus *enquiring* words and phrases that apply to their parameters.

STAGE 2

Step 4. Ask each group to take three minutes to feed back their observations to the room.

Step 5. As facilitator, pick one pair of examples from each group and write these onto a flip chart/whiteboard.

Step 6. Ask the group as a whole to discuss why they think project teams often default to the language of control.

Step 7. Ask the group what they think the impact of controlling language has on team effectiveness.

STAGE 3

Step 8. Agree what steps the group might take to improve their speech patterns when they talk in meetings but also when they communicate using email.

OTHER THOUGHTS

1. It is important to distinguish between open language and merely being polite. Polite language can be passive aggressive and is often ambiguous in its meanings.

2. Collaborative language is not about being artificially friendly. People engaged in effective dialogue need to be clear and precise in their thoughts but, crucially, must also allow space for the other party to express themselves.

TOOL 23 – BUILDING A TEAM PSYCHOMETRIC PROFILE

PURPOSE

- To improve understanding of individual personality preferences or motivation.
- To help identify communication blind spots.
- To improve inter-team dialogue.
- A good team building exercise.

Time required: 2–4 hours depending upon the choice of test and the time available.

THE THEORY

Psychometric tests involve an individual completing a questionnaire, the results of which provide an insight into their underlying mental traits and preferences in how they think. Partly genetic and partly learned, these factors influence our attitudes and actions. Whilst most psychometric tests are designed for personal development, they can also be valuable in helping team members understand each other's behaviour. The idea is to find an appropriate test that will help the team members recognize both the differences and the similarities in their preferred styles of thinking and behaving. The real value comes in the form of improved communication as the team members learn to adapt their style to improve the chances of being understood.

There is a wide range of potential psychometric tests on the market, with many companies selling their own proprietary systems. Most facilitators only bother with the expense of qualifying in one test and will tend to be heavily biased in promoting its use. It is therefore important to remember that the test chosen is for team development rather than personal growth or recruitment. It should therefore fulfil all of the criteria set out below.

- The questionnaire should be easy to complete.

- The test should be relatively cheap to administer.
- The theory and the results should be deliverable in a short workshop session of between 90 and 120 minutes.
- The results should be able to be mapped out in a single memorable diagram that can quickly be recalled in the future.

THE TOOL

Step 1. Choose an appropriate test (see below for further information).

Step 2. Find a suitably qualified facilitator to administer the test.

Step 3. Set up a workshop. This might be a session specifically to improve communication or it might form part of a longer team building session.

Step 4. Arrange for the facilitator to run though the theory of the test and reveal each person's results.

Step 5. Having allowed some time for each individual to digest their personal results, the important part of the session is to get them to identify and discuss any differences that arise. This can be done in pairs to start with then opened up to the wider group. Do not rush this stage as it is through discussion and comparison that the team start to recognize and value their differences.

Step 6. Map out every member on a chart for future reference and include the chart in the Team Integration Manual (see **Tool 20**).

OTHER THOUGHTS

1. Some psychometric tests, particularly those used in recruitment and selection, may be too personal or time consuming to be used as a team building exercise. I would

therefore recommend the use of a more 'lightweight' system, which produces results which the team members can quickly recognize in themselves and in others. As mentioned above, there are a lot of proprietary tests being promoted in the market but the two 'systems' I have found to be the most effective for a short team building exercise are SDI and Discovery Insights.

2. There is also a range of team diagnostic tools that are mainly designed to help established teams to understand more about the impact of their personal behaviours on the team environment. Examples that I have come across include the *Team Connect 360*, the *Team Diagnostic Survey* and the *Team Ei Survey*. These are all proprietary systems requiring the use of an accredited facilitator. In the context of a project team, such instruments are more useful for a team that is struggling and needs to re-establish its collaborative base.

3. I would emphasis that psychometric tests should be treated with a degree of caution. Setting aside the traits-based systems used by the psychologists, most psychometrics provide limited information about an individual. My point is that the lightweight tests I recommend above are great for encouraging a team to think about each other in a more tolerant and inquisitive way, but they are not absolute predictors of behaviour.

TOOL 24 – EVERYONE SPEAKS, EVERYONE IS HEARD

PURPOSE

- To encourage problem-solving.
- To speed up the discussion.
- To ensure full team engagement.
- To stop extroverts from dominating the discussion.
- To keep the discussion focused on the agenda.

Time required: As required to reach the objective.

THE THEORY

Meetings can frequently become dominated by two or three individuals who take over the conversation as they argue around an issue, often taking the discussion off point, reflecting their personal agendas. The effect is to hijack the meeting away from its original purpose, eating into time allotted to other parts of the agenda. Those team members not involved in the discussion tend to become bored, irritated, or simply disengaged from the meeting. Even if they do have an opinion, less extrovert members of the team may feel intimidated and therefore hesitant to express an opinion. One solution is to impose some structure on the discussion.

THE TOOL

At the start of a meeting where everyone is expected to participate, explain that the discussion will work to the following structure.

Step 1. Everyone is allocated three minutes to give their opinion on the issue. In that time *no one is allowed to interrupt them*. They do not have to use the entire three minutes but the structure requires that everyone is given the time and space to express their opinion. The rest of the team are required to actively listen to the speaker.

Step 2. After everyone has spoken, other team members are allowed to ask each other for a point of clarification but must refrain from expressing an opinion until Step 4.

Step 3. Whoever is chairing the meeting should now be able to condense or summarize the different perspectives so that the pros and cons of the potential options are clear.

Step 4. The chair now asks each team member to express their view on the potential solution. Again this is done one at a time without interruption.

You will often find that the discipline of this exercise now allows a decision to be made but, if the issue is complex, another round of expression/listening may be necessary.

OTHER THOUGHTS

It may seem that this structure is time consuming. You are likely to find, however, that by constraining the dominant personalities, the discussion remains focused on the problem that needs to be resolved. Including the quieter members of the team is likely to improve the quality of the discussion and will significantly improve team engagement. Feedback from managers who have used this technique report that, to their surprise, the meeting tends to finish more quickly than expected.

This tool comes from the brilliant book *Time to Think* by Nancy Kline. She puts a great deal of importance on the need to ensure that each person is allowed to speak without interruption. Her observation is that interruption is highly destructive to our thinking patterns. When someone interrupts us, we often get annoyed and the adrenaline 'kicks in', disrupting the formation of new ideas and connections. She makes the point that

> When people know they will have a turn and be allowed to finish their thought, they think more quickly and say less. When they anticipate interruption … they rush and they elaborate. Interruption takes up more time than allowing people to sweep cleanly through to the end of an idea. (Kline, 1999 p. 109)

See also **Tool 11** – Extrovert and introvert thinking.

TOOL 25 – SYSTEMIC PROBLEM-SOLVING MODEL

PURPOSE

- To find the root cause of a problem.
- To learn to avoid future problems.
- To avoid the tendency to develop a blame culture.

Time required: 45–60 minutes.

THE THEORY

Humans have an instinctive desire to quickly seek the cause of any problem. We subsequently ignore many of the peripheral issues that may have contributed to the situation. The outcome is to apportion blame onto the failings of an individual or external group. Taking a systemic approach prompts the team to answer a broader range of questions before coming to a conclusion. This tool encourages a dispassionate review and nudges the team to recognize the possibility of its own role in creating the problem.

THE TOOL

The tool is set out below. The questions are largely sequential but can be adapted to suit the issue under consideration. They may also be iterative so that the answers to a later question may require revisiting one of the earlier steps.

Step 1. *Clarity*: Check that this the real problem. What else lies behind it?

- What are the facts?
- What are our assumptions?
- What emotions may be affecting our judgement?

Step 2. *Understanding*: What is going on here? What is happening below the surface that we have not recognized?

Step 3. *Outcome*: What outcome do we now want to achieve?

- What is the best case?
- What is the worst case?

Step 4. *Options.*

- What are the extremes that are open to us?
- What are the three best possible solutions?

Step 5. *Implications.*

- What is likely to happen?
- Are there any unintended consequences?

Step 6. *Action*: Commit to a plan and execute.

OTHER THOUGHTS

Systemic thinking is a habit that can be acquired through practice. The starting point is to learn to recognize your emotional reaction to a problematic event and the instinct to find someone to take the blame. Remember that by focusing on blame we limit both the ability to analyse and to learn from the situation. Stepping through a series of questions helps reduce the emotional temperature and opens the group's thinking to see the broader systems that are in play.

TOOL 26 – WHO PLAYS THE FOOL?

PURPOSE

- To have someone on your team who will take on the role of watching the team's behaviours from 'all points of the compass'.
- To keep the team focused on its mission.
- To help the team think about different perspectives.
- To avoid 'Groupthink' and challenge the team to explore alternative options.

Time required: Open-ended.

THE THEORY

The role of 'the fool' has been used in many societies over the course of human history. One can identify the role in cultures as diverse as the Aztecs, the Romans, and the Dakota Indian tribes of North America. Perhaps one of the best known appears in *King Lear*, where Shakespeare uses the character of the Fool to speak truthfully to the King without fear of retribution.

In the context of a team, the role of the fool is to maintain an alternative perspective and to look at the team through a different lens. The perspectives are both from inside and outside the team, effectively examining it based on its actions, rather than what it says it is going to do. An element of this function is sometimes carried out by external consultants who gather data on a team and then feed back what they have seen and heard. What makes the role of 'team fool' different is that he or she must also observe and then comment on the emotional sides of the team's behaviours which will be both light and dark.

This is an unorthodox approach which may not work for homogenous teams who do not wish to be challenged. The role is nevertheless a potentially valuable mechanism to help a team that wishes to learn and develop.

THE TOOL

The process for establishing the role of the team fool is relatively simple whilst also potentially being quite complicated. Much depends on how the team feel about having someone being given the task of periodically making them uncomfortable. The team leader must first explain the role of the team fool, its benefits and the potential challenges it poses.

The key question is then how it will work in practice. This depends on who plays the team fool. There are three potential options.

Option 1. An individual is appointed to work alongside the team throughout its mission, but probably on a part-time basis. The person is therefore seen as part of the team but since he or she has no technical role they are not necessarily seen as being 'within' the team. The team gives the individual licence to say what they see, without fear of attack. The team fool has no direct authority and must leave the decision to act on their observations with the team and its leaders.

Option 2. Another alternative is to appoint a volunteer from within the team to act as team fool, as an additional role on the team. Humans are quite good at adopting alter egos and it can often be acceptable to the wider group for someone to adopt another persona to pass on a difficult message. A good question from the team might be, 'so what does the Fool make of this situation?' This gives the nominated fool (or anyone else in the team) the permission to articulate thoughts and observations from both the external and internal perspectives.

Option 3. As discussed in chapter 3, there is a growing interest in the role of the external team coach, who is skilled in the art of helping teams put in place the process and practice for embedding and maintaining strong team dynamics. This role is actually well suited to perform the activities required of the team fool.

OTHER THOUGHTS

If this concept is of interest then you can find more thoughts and observations in a book called *The Corporate Fool* by David Firth and Alan Leigh (2010).

TOOL 27 – THE 'SO WHAT?' MONITOR

PURPOSE

- To keep any discussions focused on the team's objective.
- To ensure that meetings and workshops conclude with an agreed set of actions.

Time required: Open-ended.

THE THEORY

Meetings have a tendency to stray away from the original purpose or agenda. This is often particularly problematic for teams exploring new areas which they have not covered before. Workshops which encourage better communication or draw out a new way of thinking can be quite exhilarating for the team. The investment in such events is, however, wasted if the new ideas and commitments are not then developed into a series of actions.

It is not uncommon for a team to spend two days at an off-site retreat doing some great work together only to revert to their original process and behaviours as soon as they return to the work place. The purpose of the 'so what?' monitor is to act as a reality check on the team's discussions and ensure they result in a practical series of actions that will move the team forwards.

Good examples of 'so what?' questions include:

1. So what has that point got to do with our objective?
2. So what have we learned from that experience?
3. So what are we going to do with that idea?

These questions help bring the discussion back to the needs of the project or initiative. This role must therefore maintain a clear link to the vision and purpose of the team. A clear vision provides the fixed point of reference or the 'guiding star' that helps answer most 'so what' questions (see **Tool 10** and **Tool 27**).

THE TOOL

Step 1. Explain to the team that the role requires the person in that role to periodically ask a number of 'so what' questions as the debate and discussion unfolds.

Step 2. At the start of the meeting/workshop ask someone to take on the role of 'so what?' monitor.

Step 3. The 'so what?' question is used towards the end of every session when a short period of time should be allowed to agree and take note of any agreed actions.

Step 4. At the end of the workshop/meeting, the 'so what?' monitor, runs through the actions list so that everyone participating in the meeting has the chance to think about what is going to happen in the future and what changes have been agreed.

OTHER THOUGHTS

1. The 'so what?' monitor is a part-time role that should be shared amongst the team so that everyone has a turn. Over time the group will learn to think in a much more focused way.
2. It should be regarded as a supportive role, rather than simply trying to be difficult. 'So what?' questions should be asked to try and open up the team's thinking rather than close it down. The tone with which the questions are asked should be enquiring rather that controlling (see **Tool 22**).

TOOL 28 – AGREE YOUR MEETING STRATEGY

PURPOSE

To make the best use of time spent in meetings.

Time required: 30 minutes.

THE THEORY

Teams need to periodically come together to connect, discuss problems and agree actions. Good meetings help re-energize a team providing direction and clearing the way to progress to the next stage. On the other hand poorly structured meetings can lead to frustration and disengagement. One of the features of bad meetings is the tendency to overfill the agenda with too many disparate items.

Meeting type	Nature of the meeting	Example Output
Progress	Regular, short and precise	Concise minutes
Technical	Ad hoc – should not involve the whole team	Technical progression or escalation
Problem-solving	Creative – should include members of the team who can offer different insights	Clear decision and then action
Strategic	Periodic – exploratory	Adjusted project execution plan
Learning	Reflective	Written summary and agreement to change

Table 6 – Meeting strategy guide

You can improve your chances of running a good meeting by agreeing a structure with the team at an early stage in the project. The table above sets out a number of common types of meeting. This list is not comprehensive and you may have others you wish to add. By agreeing a structure in advance, the team understands the principles of how the team will come together at difficult times and can organize themselves as necessary.

The analysis of meeting type will then help you form an appropriate agenda but will also help you decide who needs to attend.

THE TOOL

Step 1. Make a copy of the above table or download it from www.teamcoachingtoolkit.com/agree-meeting-strategy/

Step 2. Provide a copy of the table to the core members of your team before the next meeting and ask them to think about the types of meeting they think the team will need.

Step 3. At the meeting set out your thoughts on developing a meeting strategy and discuss with the team how to make your meetings as effective as possible.

Step 4. Having agreed the strategy write up your conclusions and include them in the Team Integration Manual (**Tool 20**).

OTHER THOUGHTS

1. Probably one of the loudest complaints from most project teams is that they spend too much time in meetings. What they actually mean is they often find themselves in the wrong types of meeting where their contribution is not needed, or perhaps not even asked for. It is easy to fall into the trap of creating something that Patrick Lencioni describes as 'meeting stew' (Lencioni, 2004). This is a multi-purpose approach to the use of meeting time, where every kind of issue is added to the agenda. To give a common example, a progress meeting is set up requiring everyone to attend. The event should be no more than a short update session but an hour later the meeting is still dragging on, as two members of the team begin arguing over an issue which is largely irrelevant

to everyone else. Having a structured approach to meetings allows you to cut off the discussion on the basis that the matter should be picked up in the appropriate session.

2. A useful pointer is to remember that every person you add to a meeting exponentially increases the time taken to reach a conclusion on each issue under discussion. So always ask yourself the question 'does everyone really need to be here?'

TOOL 29 – IDENTIFYING THE ELEPHANT

PURPOSE

To identify and mitigate a tacit, or unspoken, issue that is affecting the team's ability to perform.

Time required: 60–90 minutes depending upon the size of the elephant.

THE THEORY

The 'elephant in the room' is usually a reference to an issue or situation which is affecting the behaviour of a group or team but no one wishes to discuss. The problem may be a source of uncertainty, embarrassment, or a potential source of conflict. The issue is elephant-sized in that it is significantly large to have an impact on decision-making and teamwork. The tacit or unspoken social rules created by the team require that the issue is not mentioned, as to do so is perceived as a threat to team cohesion. Often the elephant relates to relationships either within the team or with an influential stakeholder. However, if this issue is getting in the way of the team's ability to deliver its goal, then it must be addressed and the team encouraged to talk about it.

THE TOOL

Step 1. Assess the situation and sense whether there is something affecting the dynamics of the team. This might be something specific or possibly a general sense of discomfort in certain meetings.

Step 2. Check your senses with one or two of your team to see if the issue is real.

Step 3. Once you have a greater awareness of the issue, think about how you might approach the subject. If the matter is particularly sensitive there is a potential danger in simply starting a discussion on the issue when others are unprepared. You need to have a plan as to how to steer the conversation.

Step 4. Raise the issue at the next appropriate opportunity. You might make an opening statement along the lines that you sense there is an issue that is not being discussed and that there may be an 'elephant in the room'.

Step 5. Remind the team about the importance of its mission and vision. Then ask the team 'so is there anything that we should be talking about that is currently being ignored?'

Step 6. The response will be governed by the extent to which the team feels safe enough to speak up. In a team where trust is low, you may get little or no response. It may be helpful to have primed one of your team to speak up to start the discussion. Alternatively you can move the conversation forward by stating 'I have noticed that we never talk about xxx – why is that?'

Step 7. On the presumption that you have stimulated some form of discussion on the matter you must now close the discussion around the question 'so what are we going to do about this issue so that it no longer gets in our way?'

OTHER THOUGHTS

There is, of course, a possibility that you are the 'elephant' or are somehow connected with it. As team leader you have a fundamental impact on the team dynamic and your approach or style may not be working for the team. If they lack the mechanism to discuss this, you are unlikely to get the team to talk openly about it as a group.

It is therefore good practice to ask the team for feedback about your leadership style and approach to the management of the project. If you suspect there is an issue developing, then consider asking someone on the team to run an externally administered 360 degree feedback process where the results are fed back to someone outside the team who can present them in an anonymized form, thus encouraging a more honest appraisal.

If the feedback is critical, allow yourself to move through the shock cycle as described in Tool 35 so that you can move through your initial irritation without getting stuck in the 'disbelief' stage. When you are ready, you should then decide on a strategy to adapt your approach. This requires a degree of courage and flexibility. It is worth persevering as I have heard many stories of projects that were turned around simply by the team leader recognizing they were the source of the team's ineffectiveness and then doing something about it.

TOOL 30 – PERCEPTUAL POSITIONS FROM THE 'EXTRA CHAIR'

PURPOSE

- To find an additional perspective on a problem or issue.
- To expand the mental filters of members of the team.
- To articulate points of view or concerns that are perceived to come from people/organizations not in the room.

Time required: 10 minutes.

THE THEORY

When considering a complex problem where there are multiple options and outcomes, it can be very useful to be able to take in a third party perspective. This can, however, be impractical when decisions must be made quickly to keep the programme on track and the third party is not available.

One alternative is to ask a member of the team to adopt the persona of an influential stakeholder who is not in the room and then ask them what they think. Humans are surprisingly good at removing themselves from their own personality to temporarily take on the mindset of someone they know or imagine they know. This is made easier if one physically changes position.

Often the substitute will find they can quickly tap into the primary perspectives relevant to the issue in question and can provide some insight into the problem that had not previously been included in the discussion.

THE TOOL

Step 1. When discussing a challenging issue involving people who are not present at the meeting, find a spare chair and place it at the meeting table.

Step 2. Explain to the team that whoever is sitting in that chair represents the stakeholder/ sponsor/user.

Step 3. Ask someone to physically change seats for a minute to temporarily adopt the persona or group whose views would be useful.

Step 4. Ask them to then speak on the issue or discuss that person or group's perspective.

Step 5. When they have finished, ask the substitute to take their own seat again.

Step 6. Keep the chair at the table for the rest of the discussion so that the team are aware of its presence.

OTHER THOUGHTS

If you are not familiar with the idea of creating a 'perceptual position' then this might feel a bit unusual. I recommend that you try it. You will be surprised how easy it is for the person in the chair to adopt the thought patterns and perspectives of another person or even a whole organization.

TOOL 31 – BUILDING STAKEHOLDER SUPPORT

PURPOSE

To build and maintain support from influential stakeholders.

Time required: 60 minutes.

THE THEORY

Studies on team performance highlight a consistent problem where a team has been well formed and can work together effectively and yet still fails to achieve its objective. Projects and initiatives invariably require support from sponsors and stakeholder groups. This might be in the form of resources or simply gaining access to the information needed to complete the task. Deborah Arcona and her colleagues (2002) identified the difference in outcomes achieved by teams who were able to connect with internal and external resources needed to maintain momentum compared to teams who were not.

It is a process of managing upwards and using the power of influence as and when required. This is particularly important in organizations with flat matrix management structures. Stakeholder communication and management plans are

CASE STORY

I interviewed a woman who told me how she managed to deliver a knowledge management initiative she was leading for a large multinational organization. The initiative had taken a long time to mobilize as it required the support of both regional and sector leaders from around the world. The potential benefits of establishing a full database of the organization's expertise and experience were going to be significant but success required a commitment to invest time in research, system design and communication. She knew that there was always a danger that some of the senior managers would lose interest as their attention became focused on business-as-usual and so she set up a system to try and retain their active support. Her team comprised researchers and knowledge managers from around the world and so she spent time equipping them with the information they would need to provide regular updates to their line managers and leaders, showing the progress they were making and reminding the local office

158

an essential and well-understood component of project management. For real engagement, however, it is better to establish an engagement plan based around personal relationships.

As the project cycle plays out there will be times when you need more resources, more time or simply need to ensure the organization remains committed to your project. As Arcona's studies show, you should ensure that you and your team

of the benefits they would get from having access to this global database. She believed this strategy helped ensure the project was not scrapped when the organization went through a cost reduction programme, where other programmes were mothballed or cancelled.

maintain good connections with those people who you need to keep as advocates of your endeavour. One mechanism is to ask each of the team to take on the role of ambassador, maintaining regular communication with their nominated stakeholder.

The ambassadorial role is to promote the interests of the team to those stakeholders who have an influence or an interest in the team's progress. In practice this means understanding their specific concerns, and keeping them informed of progress. The objective is to ensure that every key stakeholder becomes an active supporter of your mission. This will become particularly important when the project comes under pressure and you may need additional resources or information.

THE TOOL

Step 1. Introduce the concept of the role of ambassador to the team.

Step 2. Ask them what the role might look like.

Step 3. Build a role specification setting out the activities involved, the outcomes expected and the accountability that is attached to it (see **Tool 9**).

Step 4. Ask the team to help map out who you need to influence both inside and outside the organization.

Step 5. Allocate relationships to each member as they are best suited to build or maintain the relationship.

CHAPTER 7

TOOLS FOR BUILDING RESILIENCE

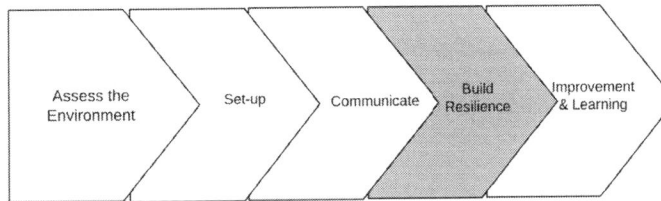

Figure 2D – Team coaching model: Build Resilience

Tool 32	Press reset
Tool 33	Taking the resilience temperature
Tool 34	Constructive challenge
Tool 35	Coping with difficult news
Tool 36	Fault-free conflict management and the 'Evil Genius'
Tool 37	Hedges and ditches
Tool 38	The pre-mortem

TOOL 32 – PRESS RESET

PURPOSE

To provide a structure for a team that is not working effectively and needs to reset its behavioural norms.

Time required: A full day workshop.

THE THEORY

'Pressing the reset button' is a useful metaphor for calling a halt to the progression of dysfunctional behaviour and starting again. Typically the need for a reset occurs when the team's interactions have defaulted to transactional behaviours and collaboration and communication has become sporadic. The situation often arises because some of the key early team development stages were missed out or rushed. The reset process is designed to encourage the team to discuss as a group what has gone wrong and what they can now do to recreate a stronger more effective team to complete the project.

PRELIMINARY WORK

It is recommended that some initial investigatory work is done. This requires talking to each of the key members of the team to understand each individual's perspective of the project, and what has happened (or not happened) to create the dysfunctional environment. Depending upon the situation, it may be useful to find an experienced facilitator who can take on the role of independent assessor.

The workshop structure will obviously be shaped by the outcome of the workshop interviews but should broadly be shaped around three stages – Reflection, Resurrection and Resilience.

THE TOOL

STAGE 1 – REFLECTION

Step 1. *Set the ground rules for the day:*

- no blame to be attributed
- everyone is required to speak and everyone must be given space to speak
- no talking over others
- be open to new ways of thinking
- be reflective
- dialogue (an exchange of views) rather than debate (the presumption that only one of a number of opposing views can be correct)

Step 2. *Reality check – why are we here?* The team leader or facilitator presents an overview of the project to date, setting out areas of collective failure and the implications on the project. Where appropriate, data collected in the preliminary research should be fed back to the team.

At this point in the day, the focus here is purely to establish the need for a change in behaviours. The team should be discouraged from apportioning blame to any individual or group inside or outside of the team. Before moving to the next stage there needs to be a clear and unambiguous answer to the question 'do you agree that a different approach is needed?' It is important that everyone verbally agrees. If necessary, ask each person in turn to respond to the question.

Step 3. *How did we get to this point?* This stage should revolve around questions such as, 'so what happened, and what was my role?' and 'how do I currently feel about the situation we are in?'

Encourage the group to distinguish between facts and feelings. This can be done using red hat and white hat thinking, where the team take part in two rounds of discussion. In the first round everyone wears an imaginary white hat and must only discuss facts and relevant events. No emotion should be expressed in this round. In the second round everyone switches to the imaginary red hat and is encouraged to talk about how they feel about the situation. Once again, it is important that everyone is allowed to make a contribution (see **Tool 24**).

The session might close with the question 'can any one of you succeed if the rest of the team fail?'

STAGE 2 – RESURRECTION

Step 4. *What would 'better' look like?* The next session requires the team to identify the hypothetical features that would be part of an effective team. You are not yet trying to address the current team's problems. Instead you are asking them to explore a wider potential pool of ideas. Some of the answers may appear obvious but you should try and avoid the temptation to go for a quick fix. It is really important that every member has a say as to what a good team looks like to them. This might be done by splitting the team into two groups and developing a set of ideas around a flip chart.

Another very powerful tool is to use story telling where the group is asked to think of a project in their past where the team worked well together. What happened and what can the team learn from that story (see **Tool 12**)?

Step 5. *What would we have to change to get there?* Ask each member of the team to take a few minutes to write down what they see as the primary challenges in completing the tasks ahead and what the others in the team could do to help them be successful in their role.

Each member then takes a turn to explain their thinking to the others around the table, without interruption. The session closes with each team member then reflecting on what they have heard and what they could do differently in future.

Step 6. *Agree a new set of Rules of Engagement.* The team should now set out a formal set of Rules of Engagement based on the output from the day and other forms of best practice. The Rules of Engagement are designed to improve the quality and effectiveness of the team's interactions, both in the project meetings and on a one-to-one basis outside of the group (see **Tool 13**).

STAGE 3 – RESILIENCE

Step 7. *Anticipating future pressure.* The session closes with the group trying to anticipate the next set of pressure points that may emerge as the project or initiative proceeds towards completion. Having identified potential problems, the question that the team must answer is 'so how will we react as a team when these problems occur?' This mechanism is a way of encouraging the team to think about the learning from the workshop. More importantly, it also establishes the protocols that can be used if the dynamics of the team start to revert to bad behaviours.

OTHER THOUGHTS

1. A successful reset requires acceptance by the whole of the team that the current team environment is not working. If one individual or group does not accept that there is a problem then the exercise will probably fail. Where there is strong inter-personal animosity between particular individuals, it may be necessary to remove one or both of them from the team. This is a tough call but inter-personal conflict is usually very difficult to resolve without a lot of work.

2. This is a workshop around behaviours and re-engagement of the team with the project. It should not be used to deal with commercial issues. If any team members have significant financial arguments with the client/sponsor, or amongst themselves, these need to be captured elsewhere beforehand and then parked.

3. The workshop should ideally be off-site in a comfortable environment. The key to success is to allow the team time to reflect and talk. The process really needs a full day to work through each of the stages. It is less likely to work if condensed into a shorter period.

4. Ideally, there should be no more than eight people around the table plus the facilitator. The process can work with more people but the dynamics of the discussion are more difficult. On large projects, it is essential that all of the key parties attend and that they have the authority to ensure that any new rules agreed at the workshop are cascaded though the sub teams.

TOOL 33 – TAKING THE RESILIENCE TEMPERATURE

PURPOSE

- To stimulate a discussion about stress when the team is under pressure.
- To give members of the team the opportunity to articulate the pressures they are experiencing.
- To allow team members to recognize the stress that may be hindering the ability of some of the other members to fulfil their role.

Time required: 10–20 minutes.

THE THEORY

All large projects are likely to come under pressure at some stage in the programme. The more complex the project, the greater the chances of change in scope, sponsor support, resourcing etc. Stress has become a 'steady state' for many people at work, in that we constantly have more tasks to do than can be achieved in the waking hours of the day. When a project is heading into a period of pressure, however, it is possible that the additional workload puts the team into a heightened sense of anxiety. This can be counterproductive. The challenge is to find a mechanism that encourages the team to pause, recognize the stresses that they are under and articulate the challenges. Pressure is not necessarily a bad thing. Deadlines and difficult problems can often be the mechanisms that bond a team together. Teams under excess pressure may, however, simply disintegrate. This tool enables the team leader to start a discussion that may pre-empt derailment and may also help build stronger bonds within the team.

THE TOOL

Step 1. At the start of the team meeting (or perhaps following a break in a meeting that has been particularly fraught) inform the team that you're going to pause the agenda for a moment to 'take the temperature of the team's resilience'.

Step 2. Whilst the team are thinking about their response, draw up a thermometer or, if you feel the artwork is beyond you, simply draw a line on a flip chart.

Step 3. Ask the question 'on a scale of 1 to 10, how resilient are you feeling *at this precise moment?*'

Step 4. Starting with a team member who you think is most likely to provide an open response, go around the table allowing each team member to speak in turn. If the team's scores are 5 or less, ask them why they are feeling low *today*.

Step 5. You can now make a judgement call as to whether you feel it will be useful to discuss what has been revealed. The default position for a typical team would be to return to the agenda of the meeting. You may, however, feel it is appropriate to encourage discussion on what steps might be taken to relieve the pressure and how others in the team might provide support or assistance.

Step 6. At the end of the meeting ask the same question again and see if there has been any improvement in the collective score. Often simply allowing the team to talk about the pressures that they are under creates an improvement in the collective sense of resilience.

OTHER THOUGHTS

- The point of asking about how the team is feeling 'at this precise moment' is to test the mood created by the pressures that are present now, rather than in the past. You are therefore asking the team to explain their current feelings, whilst they are in the group environment, rather than how they might have felt at some time when they have been working alone

- This exercise assumes that the team feel they are working in a psychologically safe environment. In other words, they are comfortable revealing feelings of possible weakness without the fear of being exposed to ridicule or sanction.

- The process obviously carries a degree of potential risk. Some team members may feel uncomfortable with the question and will simply pick a median score with little explanation as to why. There is also the possible risk that this question acts as a catalyst whereby all of the team's fears and frustrations are revealed at a time when you are not ready to manage them. The benefit, however, can be significant. If the team are prepared to open up, this tool can provide a highly effective mechanism for building a collective sense of commitment, not just to the project but also to each other.

TOOL 34 – CONSTRUCTIVE CHALLENGE

PURPOSE

- To improve the quality of discussion and thought when problem-solving.
- To avoid possible tendency towards 'Groupthink'.

Time required: Open.

THE THEORY

One of the features of an effective team is its ability to have robust and challenging discussions around a difficult topic without creating inter-personal animosity. Teams nevertheless need to learn to be comfortable with this type of challenge and so having a base mechanism for testing an idea can be helpful.

David Johnson and Roger Johnson made the important recognition that we only have a limited perception of any given situation, which is shaped by our own experiences and mental biases. They used the term 'constructive controversy' (Johnson & Johnson, 1979) to introduce a technique that works though the natural process that humans use to express and defend a position but then be open to others challenging it. The sequence is set out in figure 14.

The crucial element is an acceptance that your own ideas may not be the best possible solution, therefore being open to a degree of uncertainty. The role of the team coach is to ensure that this uncertainty is used as an opportunity to explore alternatives. Try not to allow individuals to become entrenched in a proposition as a defensive reaction to the perceived criticism of others.

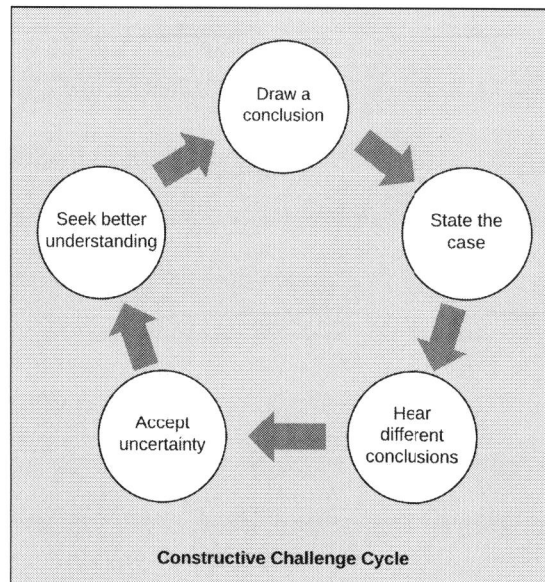

Figure 14 – Constructive challenge cycle

THE TOOL

Step 1. Agree the ground rules. This is really important as tensions can quickly rise when someone feels criticized or alternatively is uncomfortable critiquing a teammate's ideas. Be clear that the objective is to achieve what is best for the project. The team must always try and focus on conclusions based on evidence and reason rather than emotional reactions.

Step 2. Identify and summarize the problem and ask if everyone is clear on the question that needs to be answered.

Step 3. Ask each member of the team to take five to ten minutes to think by themselves about a potential solution. (Note: individuals thinking alone tend to create more ideas than would be produced by the traditional brainstorming approach.)

Step 4. Ask for the ideas and then pick out two or three of the solutions that seem to have the greatest potential.

Step 5. Ask different members of the team (or even create sub teams) to put forward a case to adopt a particular solution.

Step 6. Invite the others to make a case as to why the solution may not work, reminding everyone of the ground rules around respect and personal criticism. This may require some initial mediation as they learn how to comment and critique rather than simply find reasons as to why a suggestion may not feasible.

Step 7. Repeat Steps 5 and 6 for the other ideas.

Step 8. Now ask the individuals (or teams) to swap solutions and make a case for or against their previous positions. This is where some of the best insights are likely to arise.

Step 9. Having found a solution that makes sense to the whole team, have a short review and ask the team how they found the process. Over time, the team will learn to adopt this form of open-minded rational critique. This process eventually becomes quicker and easier requiring less structure.

CREDIT

This tool is adapted from an article 'Constructive Controversy – Improving solutions by arguing for and against your options' published in the Mind Tools suite (www.mindtools.com/pages/article/newTMC_71.htm).

TOOL 35 – COPING WITH DIFFICULT NEWS

PURPOSE

To build the capacity to help the team absorb bad news without derailing their performance.

Time required: 30–60 minutes (depending on the size of the team).

THE THEORY

When we are given bad news we often go through a range of emotions. In the context of a project this will tend to occur when an event takes place or a decision is made that is likely to have a material impact on the team's ability to deliver the required outcome.

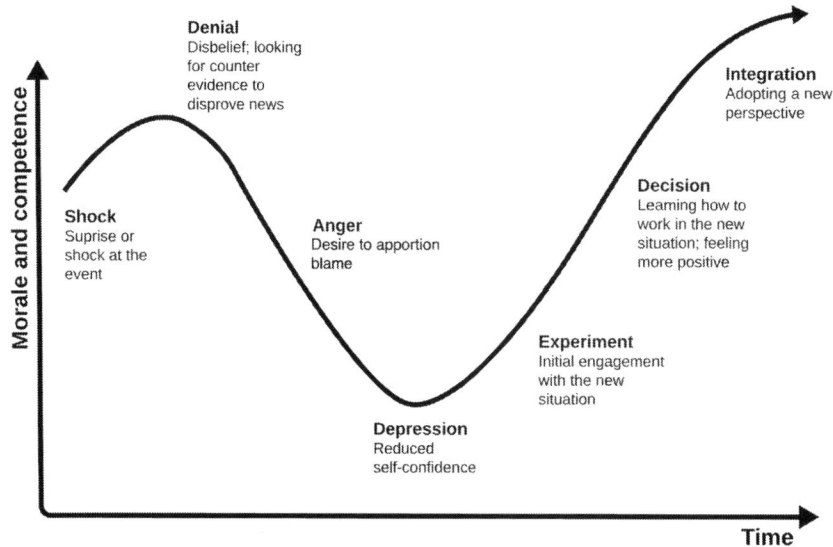

Figure 15 – Kübler-Ross change curve (Kübler-Ross, 1969)

Your objective as team leader is to pass on the information to the team and then let them move through the emotional cycle. This typically runs as shown in figure 15. The sequence was first identified by the psychiatrist Elisabeth Kübler-Ross (1969) to explain how humans often deal with news of terminal illness. The concept has subsequently been shown to apply to people receiving any message that is likely to have a significant impact on their physical or social environment.

The time taken to move through the cycle will vary depending upon the degree of severity of the news and each individual's personal reaction.

Your objective is to help the team collectively move through the cycle without getting stuck in one particular phase for too long. It is important to try and avoid falling into a blame culture. By separating the emotion from the facts you give the team the chance to control their feelings and look at the issue objectively.

The exercise must obviously be adapted to the context of the news and its impact on the team as a whole. The assumption for the simple exercise below is that the bad news is related to a timing, resourcing or performance issue. News that arises from personal tragedy will require an approach specific to that situation.

THE TOOL

Step 1. Ask the team to take a few minutes to think about the question 'do I feel threatened or angry by this news and if so why?'

Whilst there are other emotions that may affect the team, fear and anger are useful to draw out as distinct emotions. This is a personal question and so the information volunteered depends upon the familiarity and level of trust within the group. You should nevertheless invite the team to share their thoughts.

Step 2. Ask the room 'what steps can we take to improve this situation?'

Step 3. You now need to decide how you might move this discussion forward.

OTHER THOUGHTS

Moving through the cycle takes time and so do not expect this exercise to 'fix' the team immediately. The exercise should, however, allow them to feel they are able to take back a degree of control of their situation by focusing on a series of actions they now need to take.

There is likely to be a mix of reactions, ranging from distress to apparent indifference. The behaviours you will see are simply a reflection of each person's coping mechanism and how quickly they move through the cycle.

This exercise might be uncomfortable for some of the team but try and stick with the process. If you manage to get them to open up about how they are feeling, you will find this is likely to create much stronger inter-personal bonds and build the effectiveness of the team going forward.

TOOL 36 – FAULT-FREE CONFLICT MANAGEMENT AND THE 'EVIL GENIUS'

PURPOSE

To resolve conflict between team members.

Time required: 60–90 minutes.

THE THEORY

When two or more members of your team find themselves in a position of conflict you need to get them back into alignment as part of the team as quickly as possible. When the problem is a disagreement about task process, i.e. how something is done or not done, the conflict can usually be resolved quickly through discussion. When the conflict becomes personal it is usually highly disruptive to the rest of the team. The key element of this simple conflict model is to separate the emotions generated by the problem from the facts giving time for each to be expressed and acknowledged. This model comes from David Clutterbuck's excellent book *Coaching the Team at Work* (2007).

Clutterbuck identifies a contributor to many conflicts known as the 'Evil Genius' (Clutterbuck, 2007). This hypothetical character escalates the problem by placing a negative interpretation on the other parties' actions and obscuring the parties' ability to behave rationally. The team coach's role is to help the parties recognize the presence of the Evil Genius. This recognition can then act as a mechanism for them moving into a process of dialogue. Identifying this third party allows the others to separate fact from emotion and regain a rational perspective.

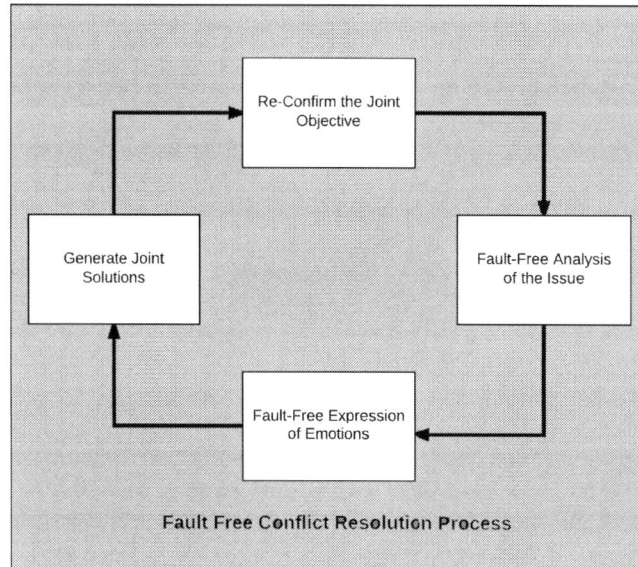

Figure 16 – Fault-free conflict resolution process

THE TOOL

Step 1. Ensure that both parties have had a period of reflection before arranging a resolution meeting.

Step 2. At the start of the meeting explain the likely presence of the Evil Genius and the role it has had in escalating the conflict that must now be resolved so that the team can go about its business. Both parties are asked, for the purpose of this process, to leave all fault with the Evil Genius.

Step 3. Explain the sequence that is going to follow as set out in figure 16.

Step 4. Reiterate the team's goals and objectives and ask both parties to respond as to whether they remain committed to them. On the assumption they both agree you now have a mandate to seek agreement.

Step 5. Each party in turn is asked to disconnect from any emotional baggage and to explain what they perceive to have happened, being clear that no fault or blame is to be attributed. The sequence works along the lines of:

- what is each person trying to achieve and why?
- why are they having difficultly (but not whose fault it is)?
- what problems the situation is creating for others?

Step 6. Ask each party to now reconnect to their emotional selves and reveal:

- how they want to feel?
- how they actually feel?
- what is making them feel the way they do?

Step 7. Ask each party if they believe they could resolve part of the other person's problem, encouraging them where possible to be generous.

Step 8. Obtain a commitment to any actions each party has offered to take to assist the other and to resolve the issue.

OTHER THOUGHTS

At first glance, this may appear to be a long-winded method of encouraging two people to settle their differences. Do not be tempted to fall into the trap of expecting people in dispute to be reasonable. When emotions run high, rational thought is suppressed. The value in the above process is that it provides a mechanism to divert the feelings of anger and frustration and to allow both parties to refocus on their longer term needs.

TOOL 37 – HEDGES AND POTHOLES

PURPOSE

- To encourage the team to anticipate the future, identify and then discuss potential problems.
- To draw out any concerns or worries individuals may have about the task ahead.

Time required: 30–60 minutes.

THE THEORY

When a team is first starting a project, or is moving into a new iteration, it can be useful to encourage them to look forward and think about the challenges ahead, without going into a full risk evaluation process.

Encouraging the group to anticipate the future before the task gets underway gives you the opportunity to understand how they regard the potential problems ahead. By having this conversation before the team comes under pressure you have a better chance of creating a blame-free discussion without any of the team withdrawing or becoming defensive.

It is useful to make the distinction between problems ahead that can be seen (hedges) and those that cannot yet be seen but might occur given the circumstances of the project (potholes). Hedges are problems that can be anticipated. Understanding the nature of the problem gives you a chance to take the necessary steps that will allow you to climb over them without getting stuck. Potholes on the other hand are potential problems that can be avoided, provided you look where you are going.

You are initially looking to draw out fears and concerns and then stimulate a discussion on potential mitigating actions. Who might be a pessimist and who may be unduly complacent?

This is a form of risk management but the exercise should avoid going too deeply into technical problems. By keeping the discussion at a more generic level you can encourage all of the team to think about their collective challenges.

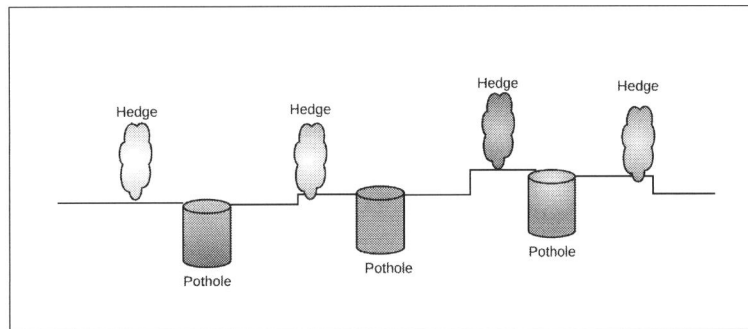

Figure 17 - Hedges and potholes

THE TOOL

Step 1. Draw a simple diagram on a flip chart similar to that shown in figure 17.

Step 2. Explain the purpose of the exercise and the benefit of thinking about potential issues now when the environment is relatively calm.

Step 3. Explain the difference between the hedges, that can be seen and are quite likely to occur, and the potholes, which are less visible, but may take the team by surprise.

Step 4. Ask the team to each take a couple of minutes to list out any hedges they can see.

Step 5. Build a list of the 'hedges' but don't at this stage discuss any solutions.

Step 6. Now ask the team to think about possible potholes. The point of separating the two exercises is to allow the hedges and potholes concept to stimulate deeper thinking.

Step 7. Now list the 'potholes'.

Step 8. The length of the two lists will vary according to the scale and complexity of the project. Ask the team to consider 'what can we do to get over the hedges and what will we do if we come across any of the potholes you have identified?'

Depending upon the number of people present, you might have one discussion or split the room into groups of three or four.

Step 9. Note the output and circulate shortly after the meeting.

OTHER THOUGHTS

This exercise is broadly similar to some of the risk identification exercises set out elsewhere in the toolkit. This process is probably more suited to smaller teams working on initiatives with a relatively short duration where formal risk management procedures would be too cumbersome.

TOOL 38 – THE PRE-MORTEM: AN ALTERNATIVE APPROACH TO RISK MANAGEMENT

PURPOSE

To use the thinking power of the wider team to anticipate problems ahead.

Time required: 2 hours.

THE THEORY

If you work on projects you are probably familiar with the idea of the 'lessons learned' workshop, where those involved in the project come together to talk about what went well, and in particular what problems could have been avoided (see **Tool 44**). The idea is to take the learning from one project or iteration into the next project. The exercise is effectively a 'post mortem'. The only problem is that this thinking goes on too late to help the project that has just been completed. So wouldn't it be useful to do a 'lessons learned' exercise **before** the project was completed, when you had a chance to do something about it? What if you did a 'pre-mortem'?

The idea a of pre-mortem has been around for a while, with a lot of the credit going to Professor Gary Klein, who raised the idea in an article in the *Harvard Business Review* (2007). Whilst a pre-mortem could be seen as another form of risk management there is a key difference. Traditional risk management exercises are a rational process, based on an extrapolation of local sequences of events. A pre-mortem allows the participants to move beyond rational thinking and articulate concerns for which they may have no clear evidence but are nevertheless potentially very real to the project participants.

This is not about finding the wackiest potential risks but instead using the 'wisdom of crowds'. A variety of studies have shown that collecting answers from a wide variety of people can produce better information than relying solely on the opinions of experts. The beauty of the process is that it engages everyone in the wider team and asks them to provide some input in areas outside of their specific area of technical expertise.

THE TOOL

The tool is best illustrated by the following extended case story.

CASE STORY

There are many ways of asking groups of people to identify problems but I offer an example of a workshop in which I took part, which gives you an idea of the process. To give some context, this was a project to create a new facility for an educational institution. It was therefore complex in design and delivery and required a highly collaborative approach from all of the team members.

The pre-mortem session was part of a quarterly collaboration workshop which was attended by 38 people, ranging from contractors and subcontractors through to the university's operations and maintenance staff. At the time of the workshop we were roughly halfway through the construction of the building.

The session started with an introduction explaining the concept and asking the team to 'get gloomy'. They were directed to shut their eyes and imagine a scenario where they were talking to a colleague some time after the project had been completed and, instead of feelings of pride in the project, they felt sad. Something had gone wrong. So what had happened? After a couple of minutes each participant was asked to write their thoughts, worries and concerns on a Post-it note, using a different Post-it for each issue.

The room was set up in banquet style with five or six people at each table. Around the room I had fixed sheets of paper on the wall for each table upon which to stick their Posts-it as they were generated. Some tables produced 15 or more ideas but every table managed to identify at least eight.

Each team member was given two votes which they could use by marking a cross on the issues that they felt were most relevant. The participants were then directed to go around the room and read the other group's issue sheets. They were given one more vote for each sheet. After a fairly chaotic 15 minutes, everyone settled back down at their table and each table was asked to pick the issue on their particular sheet which had the most votes. A group discussion took place to identify what actions should be put in place to avoid their chosen problem occurring. They were given 10 minutes to discuss, after which a nominated spokesperson was asked to feed back to the room.

This session took about an hour and a quarter. With more time, we would have done another round of issues but as it was we left the session with an action that every issue would be noted and circulated to the participants.

Was it worth the effort? Well, we identified a major potential communication gap between the main contract and the fitting-out programme, as well as a number of other pertinent risks that had not previously been articulated. Perhaps the greatest benefit to me was to see collaboration working in action, as I watched every member of this very diverse team actively engage with each other in earnest discussion for the benefit of the project. So if you are looking for an alternative to the traditional risk management process, or a simple mechanism for reinvigorating the collaborative spirit, give the pre-mortem a try. After all, what is the worst that could happen?

CHAPTER 8

TOOLS FOR ENCOURAGING LEARNING, INNOVATION AND IMPROVEMENT

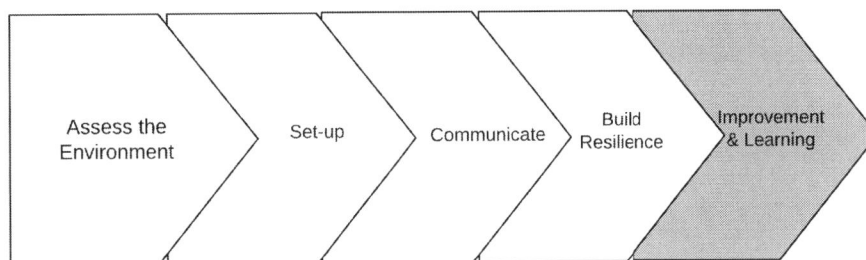

Figure 2E – Team coaching model: Improvement and Learning

Tool 39	The midpoint review
Tool 40	Knowledge stocktake
Tool 41	Capturing the knowledge
Tool 42	How are we performing?
Tool 43	Lifting the barriers to allow creative thinking
Tool 44	Running a 'lessons learned' workshop
Tool 45	Purposeful closure

TOOL 39 – THE MIDPOINT REVIEW

PURPOSE

To take advantage of a team's natural tendency to pause at the midpoint of its cycle and reset the team's process and behaviours.

Time required: A half or full day (depending upon the size of the team and the complexity of the project).

THE THEORY

A number of studies into team effectiveness have noted that many teams have a natural point roughly midway through their task or project when they are open to a period of collective review of their progress to date. At this moment they are able to pause and recognize the need to make adjustments in the way they work. The recognition of this natural midpoint was identified by Connie Gersick (1988), a professor of Human Resources and Organizational Behaviour at UCLA.

Gersick studied a wide range of teams engaged in a project or initiative and she noted that almost all went through a significant transition at the midpoint. She observed a range of

CASE STORY

A good example of a midpoint review concerns a team involved in the design and implementation of a new set of operating procedures required to comply with some substantial changes in the regulation of a financial institution. The project was programmed to be implemented over nine months and the team were aware that everything had to be in place on the date a new statute came into effect. After a slow start, the cross-functional team began to work out the scope and scale of the task. With four months to go, the team leader set up a review session. This involved all of the team as well as the sponsor and some key stakeholders. They spent time thinking about how effectively they were working as a unit and also identified a number of issues that were getting in their way. The outcome was very successful. The team felt they were now ready to pick up the pace. They were able to launch the training and implementation plan ahead of the schedule and the new systems became operational a week before the deadline.

changes, where old patterns of behaviour stopped and the teams adopted a new approach and attitude to the tasks ahead.

THE TOOL

Step 1. Consider when your team's midpoint may be. This might be time based or even task based.

Step 2. Arrange a midpoint review session. This might be a half or even a full day depending upon the size of the project team and the nature of the project.

Step 3. Decide on the agenda that you would like to cover and who will take on the role of facilitator. This is a thinking session so try not to overcrowd the agenda.

Step 4. As the first item on the agenda reaffirm the vision and mission. The purpose is to make it clear as to why this session is taking place.

Step 5. Ask each member of the team to take a few minutes to think by themselves about what has happened over the first half of the project. They should first consider what the team has done well, not just in task completion but more importantly in how the members have worked together. Depending upon the size of the team, break them into small groups so that everyone has to make an active contribution. Ask the groups to discuss the question amongst themselves and then feed back into the room.

Step 6. Repeat the process, this time to consider what has not gone so well (being careful to ensure that your no blame rules are in place – see **Tool 19**).

Step 7. Ask the team to now identify the learning that should be taken into the second half of the project. This should comprise three lists:

1. those things that we need to do more often
2. those things we could do better
3. those things that we must stop doing

Step 8. Write up, disseminate and save the conclusions in the Team Integration Manual (**Tool 20**).

TOOL 40 – KNOWLEDGE STOCKTAKE

PURPOSE

- To understand the strengths and weaknesses in the team's knowledge base.
- To establish the concept of becoming a learning team.

Time required: 60–120 minutes (depending upon the size of the team).

THE THEORY

Teams are assembled over time to achieve a specific goal. The basis for selection is usually on availability as much as it is around expertise and experience. The more complex the task, the more likely it is that there will initially be gaps in the team's knowledge and capability.

Assessing the team's capability early in the team's life cycle will improve the chances of building, or finding, the knowledge you need to fill any gaps. The exercise is also useful for checking any assumptions you might have made as to exactly who knows what.

THE TOOL

Step 1. Include an item called 'knowledge stocktake' on the agenda of an early team meeting.

Step 2. Explain the concept outlined above and the value of gaining an early understanding of the team's collective knowledge.

Step 3. Ask each of the team 'what knowledge or experience do you think you can bring to the project/initiative?'

Step 4. Ask 'what knowledge or experience do you think may be missing that is critical to our mission?'

Step 5. Ask 'who do you know or where can we go to fill in the gaps?'

Step 6. Agree how the team should record and save the output from this session so that it can help those who may join the team at some time in the future (see **Tool 41**).

OTHER THOUGHTS

Knowledge is an ethereal concept. We cannot see inside a person's head to check exactly what they know or do not know and, in a changing world, information can rapidly become redundant. At the same time, access to information via the internet means that we can quickly get up to speed on almost any technical issue. The skill is to build a mindset in the team where it is less about knowing all of the answers and more about knowing where to look.

TOOL 41 – CAPTURING THE KNOWLEDGE

PURPOSE

- To identify and capture knowledge learned by the team.
- To create an easily accessible place to save, store and maintain information that the members of the team need to deliver their mission.

Time required: 4–8 hours to set up and then ongoing maintenance.

THE THEORY

Teams engaged on a complex task will generate a wide range of data, information and knowledge that would be of significant value to other members of the team, particularly those elements that are periodic or repetitive. The knowledge learned tends to remain in people's heads rather than being written down or recorded for use by others at a later date.

There are a number of reasons why useful information fails to be captured. The most common problem is that the team becomes too focused on short-term task delivery without considering the potential efficiencies to be gained in the future. Knowledge capture is therefore a mindset issue, which should be addressed as one of the team's behavioural norms at the start of the project cycle.

A more practical problem is creating a suitable place to store information that is easy to both save and then access. There are a variety of technologies available, ranging from shared folders using an application such as Dropbox or Microsoft SharePoint. These applications are folder-based systems which work well with a limited amount of data. As the volume of folders expands, they can, however, become difficult to navigate if the folder structure if not effectively policed. An alternative approach is provided by the tool below.

A POSSIBLE TOOL

My current favourite is an application called MethodGrid which was written specifically to help organizations and teams manage their knowledge. The program has the following features:

- It is a web-based knowledge storage solution, making it easy for the team to access key knowledge and information from wherever they are based.
- Once you have decided the framework, it is easy to set up the structure.
- The program allows you to create knowledge grids which align with your process. Each grid then holds a series of elements. These are 'boxes' in which you can save all of the information and data including text, internal and external links, files and tagged experts.

You can find more information at www.methodgrid.com

NOTE: I SHOULD POINT OUT THAT I HAVE NO COMMERCIAL OR FINANCIAL INTEREST IN THIS PRODUCT. I WAS, HOWEVER, INVOLVED IN THE BETA TESTING.

TOOL NO. 42 – HOW ARE WE PERFORMING? – TEAM KEY PERFORMANCE INDICATORS

PURPOSE

To track a team's perceptions of their ability to work as a cohesive unit.

Time required: A day to set up and then 2–4 hours a month to collect, analyse and report the data.

THE THEORY

When discussing the challenges of soft issues, the conversation can quickly get lost as people struggle to articulate problems where the root cause is poor behaviour. It is therefore good practice to periodically ask every member of the team to take part in a short feedback exercise to monitor how the team feel they are progressing and where attention may need to be paid to correct areas that are causing a problem.

The structure of the feedback can be designed around a number of measures which then form part of the team's key performance indicators. The question is what to measure. Table 7 sets out 12 possible indicators that have been found in studies on teams to be leading indicators of strong team performance. By using a scale of 1 to 10, each question allows the respondent to allocate a high or low score depending upon the extent to which they agree with the comments.

The team must agree that taking these measures is important, as the process only works effectively when data is provided by the majority of the members. The value is in being able to monitor trends and see what is changing as the programme plays out over a period of time.

High Score	Behavioural Indicator	Low score
The strategy for delivering this project is absolutely clear to me	**Clear strategy**	I am not at all sure as to how we are going to deliver this project
The culture of the team encourages open admission of weaknesses and mistakes	**Trust**	It is dangerous to admit to making a mistake in this team
I feel that the team consistently treat each other respectfully	**Respect**	There are many occasions when team members act disrespectfully towards each other
I am clear on the roles and responsibilities that each member of the team plays in the delivery of this project	**Roles and responsibilities**	I am often uncertain as to who is responsible for issues that fall outside of each team member's professional remit
I see a culture in the team of trying to learn from problems rather than apportion blame	**'No blame' culture**	I see an instinctive reaction in many of the team to blame others when problems arise
I feel fully informed on all of the important decisions affecting the project	**Communication**	I feel that I am not kept up to speed on important issues
The systems and processes for sharing all relevant information are clear and well established	**Sharing information**	Information sharing is ad hoc and unstructured
The culture of the team encourages me to take the initiative to try to solve problems	**Encouraging initiative**	The suggestion of alternative forms of action is not encouraged on this project
I often see examples of flexibility in the team's approach	**Flexibility of approach**	The team is rigid in its approach to the resolution of problems
I believe the management team are committed to adopting collaborative strategies	**Client commitment to integrated working**	The actions of the senior management indicate they have little faith in creating an integrated team

High Score	Behavioural Indicator	Low score
I believe the team are all committed to a single one team ethos	One team ethos	I see the team as a group of specialists who work independently of each other
All of our meetings are compelling, well-structured and productive	Meetings	Most of our meetings are poorly structured and produce inconclusive outcomes

Table 7 – Examples of Key Performance Indicators found to have an impact on team behaviour

THE TOOL

Step 1. Agree the principle of measuring behavioural Key Performance Indicators (KPIs) with the team.

Step 2. Decide on the method of data collection that is appropriate for the size of the team. For a team of less than 20 use a spreadsheet or a simple online tool such as Survey Monkey. For larger groups consider a proprietary system such as RADAR (see www.resolex.com).

Step 3. Agree the cycle of monitoring i.e. weekly or monthly.

Step 4. Working with the team, agree which behavioural KPIs will provide a useful measure of your performance. You can download a copy of the above table from http://www.teamcoachingtoolkit.com/performing-team-performance-kpis/

Step 5. Agree who is going to administer the questionnaire and how the data will be reported back.

Step 6. When the first report is complete discuss the results with the team and agree what action might be necessary.

Step 7. Implement the agreed actions.

Step 8. Repeat the cycle to an agreed schedule of dates.

OTHER THOUGHTS

1. It typically takes about three months before people become comfortable with the feedback process. The first two cycles may therefore produce data that offers little insight, so be prepared to stay with the process. It is the trends in the data which will give you the 'hard' data around which to discuss 'soft' issues.

2. On longer projects, you need to be aware of the potential for 'feedback fatigue' in the team. Interest in providing the same data month after month may diminish over time. It is therefore worth monitoring the contribution rate so that you can take steps to rejuvenate interest when necessary. Sustaining interest will depend upon how the data is fed back to the team and the extent to which they feel their feedback is being noticed. Failure to do anything with the feedback will be highly demotivating to those who have made the effort to contribute.

3. As the project relationship moves through the programme, the key indicators may need to change. Don't be afraid to adjust some of the measures that are no longer useful. At the end of each iteration or stage of the project your review procedure should also include a look at the KPIs data.

TOOL 43 – LIFTING THE BARRIERS TO ALLOW CREATIVE THINKING

PURPOSE

To remove the blocks a team puts in place which inhibit creative thinking.

Time required: 10 minutes.

THE THEORY

When faced with the need to find a creative solution to an existing problem, many people have a tendency to initially focus on the immediate barriers to change and do not look beyond them to think how new possibilities might emerge. There is often an urge to express the view 'that will never work because….'

This instinctive reaction inhibits the ability to think creatively about the potential of a new idea and how it might be developed into a practical plan of action. Most of these immediate barriers can be overcome with some thought but, unless the team can sense the long-term benefits, they will not make the necessary effort to find a solution.

The process set out below requires the team to imagine what would happen if the immediate blockage or barrier were no longer an issue, freeing them to test out new ideas, identify their benefits and find a compulsive reason to make the best solution work.

THE TOOL

Step 1. When discussing ideas and options, be alert for the tendency of someone to quickly identify the immediate barriers that will stop a good idea being implemented.

Step 2. Ask the team to pause and imagine for a minute that they have a fairy godmother who has the power to temporarily make the barrier disappear.

Step 3. Now that the barrier is no longer there, encourage the team to continue to work through the idea and fill out the actions needed to make it work.

Step 4. Having now established a more compulsive reason for pursuing the idea, explain that the fairy godmother can no longer hold the barrier back so it has returned as an obstacle to your progress.

Step 5. Now focus on the barrier and using a problem-solving tool such as a Force field analysis (see **Tool 8**) work out a plan as to how to get around it.

OTHER THOUGHTS

This very simple mechanism works by pushing the team's time horizon beyond the immediate tasks and issues that absorb most of their mental bandwidth. Most of our day-to-day thinking occurs in the left hemisphere of the brain which deals with logic and rational process. By taking the short-term issues away you are able to nudge their thinking into the right hemisphere which is where we begin to see new concepts and alternative possibilities.

TOOL 44 – RUNNING A SUCCESSFUL 'LESSONS LEARNED' SESSION

PURPOSE

- To gain a deeper understanding of the experiences gained over the course of a project.
- To build organizational knowledge.

Time required: A half day or full day (depending upon the size of the team and/or project).

THE THEORY

Studies on adult learning highlight the value of taking time to think about recent experiences, reflect on what happened and explore alternative courses of action. For organizations to adapt to new environments, using the learning gained from recent experiences is likely to be of more practical benefit than trying to import new business models introduced by external consultants.

'Lessons learned' workshops have been shown in studies to be a highly effective mechanism to build individual and corporate knowledge, particularly when done as a group. Research shows that adults are most ready to reflect and learn at the end of a project or an iteration of the project. However, left to ourselves, we often do not take the time to properly think through the issues beyond our most immediate experiences.

A 'lessons learned' session is very different from debriefing. Debriefing is a highly effective way of making tactical improvements. It is, however, an exercise focused on how to improve a particular process or task. 'Lessons learned' is a deeper process where the team works together to explore important events that have occurred over the course of a project. Time needs to have passed so that any strong emotions have subsided and the team is able to take a more objective view.

THE TOOL

Step 1. Prework. Towards the end of the project (or a phase of the project) organize a 'lessons learned' workshop ideally giving everyone sufficient notice to ensure attendance. Where possible request attendance from members who may have left the team part of the way through as their tasks were complete. Building attendance is easier if you have gained commitment from the team at the start (see Other Thoughts below).

Step 2. A week before the session create a very simple questionnaire and send it out to each member of the team. Ask them to briefly set out the key issues they believe should be covered.

Step 3. Based on the responses, create an agenda of three to five points of discussion depending upon the time available.

Step 4. Open the workshop with clear agreement that the session should be a thinking environment (see **Technique 2**) and can only work on the basis that it is 'blame free' (see **Tool 19**).

Step 5. For each issue work through the following questions:

- what happened?
- why did it work/not work?
- what were the wider circumstances / influences?
- could we have handled the situation differently?
- what else was learned from this experience?

Step 6. To close the session ask the team 'so if we were starting this project again today what would you do to set it up for success?'

Step 7. Agree how the learning from this session will be captured and disseminated through your organization.

OTHER THOUGHTS

A study by Patricia Carrillo and her colleagues (2013) concluded that whilst many organizations have the protocols and methodologies set up to carry out 'lessons learned' exercises most are very poor at implementing them. There are many practical reasons for this including time pressure, team availability and a lack of management support. My own observation is that a 'lessons learned' exercise is too often picked up by the project leader as an afterthought and is not part of the project planning process. Since the typical 'lessons learned' exercise happens at the end of a project or initiative, it is of little direct benefit to the project and is not given sufficient priority.

The answer is to gain agreement at the start of the project that everyone will take part in a 'lessons learned' session at an agreed future date. By gaining commitment in advance, you have a much better chance of establishing the event as a successful mechanism to close off the project cycle.

TOOL 45 – PURPOSEFUL CLOSURE

PURPOSE

- To bring the team to a structured closure as the project cycle reaches completion.
- To ensure the team move onto their next roles with a healthy mental approach.

Time required: 90–120 minutes.

THE THEORY

Projects typically have a finite time span and once the objective has been reached the team must disband and move onto the next job or role.

The context of the ending will be different for each team. On many projects individuals will drift away as their role diminishes. Other projects will come to an abrupt halt. Whatever the scenario, it is worth understanding that humans are tribal by nature. We often forge strong attachments to others in the team particularly when the project has been through periods of intense pressure. It is important to allow the team to move through a process of acknowledging the end of the project and allowing each member to say or do those activities that will allow them to emotionally accept the need to close one iteration of their lives and move onto the next.

THE TOOL

There is no clear-cut sequence of actions to follow in ending a project as it will depend upon the specific circumstances of the project. My recommendation is that you consider adopting the following sequence to suit your situation.

Step 1. Organize a close out meeting designed wherever possible as some form of celebration. Even if the project has somehow failed, the process of closure is important.

Step 2. Provide a summary of the project from your perspective and talk about your personal highs and lows.

Step 3. Going around the room ask each team member what they will remember from this project.

Step 4. Ask the team how they intend to keep in touch. This might be a future reunion, staying connected through social media or simply an exchange of details. This is important as it provides a sense that there will be some form of reconnection in the future.

Step 5. Close the session by asking each member to use one word to describe their team experience.

Step 6. Hand out the box of tissues (optional).

Step 7. Go to the pub (not optional).

SECTION FOUR

What Next?

CHAPTER 9

READING LIST AND OTHER RESOURCES

READING LIST

If you are hungry for more information around the field of team coaching, here are five books that I would recommend you read.

Leadership Team Coaching by Peter Hawkins	This book provides a great foundation for new team coaching practitioners. The focal point of the book is a model based around five core disciplines. This creates a structure around which the author provides a range of insights into team dynamics and development. Recommended for experienced coaches wanting to step up to team coaching.
Coaching the Team at Work by David Clutterbuck	An excellent introduction into the concept of real teamwork and how coaching interventions work, in theory and in practice. There is a strong emphasis on helping the team learn together and building organization knowledge. Recommended for managers seeking to adopt a team coaching style of leadership.
Coaching Agile Teams by Lyssa Adkins	Whilst much of Lyssa's writing focuses on activities in the software industry she provides some great insights into coaching project teams. The book also provides a good explanation of 'Agile' as a methodology. If you are uncertain as to how 'Agile' might work in the context of your team this book is definitely worth a look. Recommended for project managers working in any industry who are interested in shifting their management philosophy.

Performance Coaching for Complex Projects by Tony Llewellyn	Published as part of the Advances in Project Management series, this book was written to introduce project managers to the best practice thinking around team performance, when working in complex environments. Recommended for project managers and leaders of cross-functional teams who recognize a need for a step change when dealing with complexity.
The Wisdom of Teams by Jan R. Katzenbach and Douglas Smith	A book used by most writers on team development as the base reference point for defining teamwork. The authors provide a clear definition of what a real team is and why an effective team takes time to evolve. Illustrated with some interesting case stories, this book will help you gain a deeper understanding of team dynamics and the types of activity that impact on how they perform. Recommended for anyone interested in understanding the basics of team development.

OTHER RESOURCES

I would also highly recommend that you check out a podcast called 'The Team Coaching Zone'. The host, Krister Lowe, has assembled a wide array of guests, all of whom have a distinct area of expertise around the development of teams. It is worth working through the whole of the back catalogue, as every podcast has something of interest.

You can find a link at www.teamcoachingzone.com/

WEBSITE

Finally remember to periodically visit teamcoachingtoolkit.com to find additional resources including articles and videos on how to build brilliant teams.

REFERENCES

Adkins, L. (2010) *Coaching Agile Teams: A Companion for ScrumMasters, Agile Coaches and Project Managers in Transition*. Addison Wesley, Boston.

Arcona, D., Bresman, H. & Kaeufer, K. (2002) 'The Comparative Advantage of X-Teams', *MIT Sloane Management Review*, 43 (3), pp. 33–39.

Bass, B.M. (1990) *Bass & Stogdill's Handbook of Leadership: Theory, Research & Managerial Applications*. Free Press, New York.

Beck, K., Beedle, M., Bennekum, A., van Cockburn, A., Cunningham, W., Fowler, M., Grenning, J., Highsmith, J., Hunt, A., Jeffries, R., Kern, J., Marick, B., Martin, R.C., Mellor, S., Schwaber, K., Sutherland, J. and Thomas D. (2001) *Agile Manifesto*. Available from agilemanifesto.org/.

Carrillo, P., Ruikar, K., & Fuller, P. (2013) 'When Will We Learn? Improving Lessons Learned Practice in Construction', *International Journal of Project Management*, 31 (4), pp. 567–578.

Clutterbuck, D. (2007) *Coaching The Team at Work*. Nicholas Brearley International, London.

Earley, C. and Mosakowski, E. (2000) 'Creating Hybrid Team Cultures: An Empirical Test of Transnational Team Functioning', *The Academy of Management Journal*, 43 (1), pp. 26–49.

Firth, D. & Leigh, A. (2010) *The Corporate Fool*. Available from www.davidfirth.com.

Gersick, C. (1988) 'Time and Transition in Work Teams: Toward a Model of Group Development', *Academy of Management Journal*, 31 (1), pp. 9–41.

Greenleaf, R. (1970) *The Servant as Leader*. Center for Applied Studies, Cambridge, Mass. Available from www.greenleaf.org/products-page/the-servant-as-leader/

Janis, Irving L. (1972) *Victims of Groupthink*. New York: Houghton Mifflin. Available from www.psysr.org/about/pubs_resources/groupthink overview.htm.

Jarche, H. (2015) 'The Triple-A Organisation and PKM', *Wirearchy: Sketches for the Future of Work,* ed. Jon Husband. Available from: wirearchy.com/wirearchy-the-ebook/

Johnson, D.W. & Johnson, R.T. (1979) 'Conflict in the Classroom: Controversy and Learning', *Review of Educational Research*, 49 (1), pp. 51–69.

Kahneman, D. (2011) *Thinking, Fast and Slow*. Penguin, London.

Katzenbach, J.R. & Smith, D. (1993) *The Wisdom of Teams: Creating the High-Performance Organization*. Harper Business School Press, New York.

Klein, G. (2007) 'Performing a Project Premortem', *Harvard Business Review* (September).

Kline, N. (1999) *Time to Think: Listening to Ignite the Human Mind*. Cassell Illustrated, London.

Kübler-Ross, E. (1969) *On Death and Dying*. Scribner, New York.

Lencioni, P. (2004) *Death by Meeting, A Leadership Fable About Solving the Most Painful Problem in Business*. Jossey-Bass, San Francisco.

Lewin, K. (1951) *Field Theory in Social Science: Selected Theoretical Papers* ed. Dorwin Cartwright. Harper & Row, New York.

Llewellyn, T. (2015) *Performance Coaching for Complex Projects*. Routledge, London.

McGuire, J.B. and Tang, V. (2011) 'Slow Down to Speed Up', Forbes Online. Available from www.forbes.com/2011/02/23/slow-down-speed-efficiency-leadership-managing-ccl.html.

References

Mind Tools Editorial Team (May 2017) 'Constructive Controversy'. Available from www.mind-tools.com/pages/article/newTMC_71.htm.

Perry, E.E. Jr., Karney, D.F. & Spencer, D.G. (2012) 'Team Establishment of Self-Managed Work Teams: A Model from the Field'. *Team Performance Management* 19 (1–2), pp. 87–108.

Schein, E. (2013) *Humble Inquiry: The Gentle Art of Asking instead of Telling.* Berrett-Koehler, San Francisco.

Sibbet, D. (2010) *Visual Meetings: How Graphics, Sticky Notes and Idea Mapping Can Transform Group Productivity.* John Wiley & Sons, New Jersey.

Stacey, R.D. (2003) *Strategic Management and Organisational Dynamics: The Challenge of Complexity*, Prentice Hall, Harlow.

Tuckman, B. (1965) 'Developmental Sequence in Small Groups', *Psychological Bulletin* 63 (6), pp. 384–399.

West, M. (2011) *Effective Teamwork: Practical Lessons from Organizational Research.* John Wiley & Sons, London.

Printed in Great Britain
by Amazon